REVISE YOUR
HIGHER
MATHEMATICS

Revised Higher

by

James G.C. Reid

© *James G.C. Reid, 1993.*
ISBN 0 7169 6012 5

ROBERT GIBSON · Publisher
17 Fitzroy Place, Glasgow, G3 7SF.

INTRODUCTION

This book is designed to show the necessary steps involved in solving problems in Higher Mathematics.

At this level of Mathematics, it is important that you show an understanding of the mathematics involved in solving a problem and this is best shown in an exam by your working. For this reason it is essential that all appropriate working is shown in an exam. You should find this book suitable for this purpose.

To gain the most benefit from this book, you are advised to read the notes at the start of each section and then attempt the worked examples which follow, before looking at the solutions.

GRAPHIC CALCULATORS

Although an excellent classroom resource, graphics calculators have no real benefit to pupils sitting Revised Higher Mathematics except for 'checking' your answers.

It would be unfair if a pupil having bought or having access to one of these machines has an advantage over a pupil who does not. Close examination of the past Revised Higher Papers shows a definite trend towards a 'graphics calculator proof' paper.

An important aspect of the examination is to show **all** your working — the reasoning behind this book is just that! To explain the important facts needed and give many worked examples of the type of questions that you may be asked.

You may use a graphics calculator in your exam **but** you must remember the above statement and SHOW ALL WORKING.

Until every pupil has their own or access to a graphics calculator they have **no part** to play in our examination system.

CONTENTS

3

SECTION 1   ALGEBRA

1.1 FUNCTIONS AND SETS

1.1.1 SETS

It is important in mathematics to clearly state what numbers you are allowed to use.

Mathematically we do this by stating the **set of numbers** that are in use.

Some commonly used number sets are listed below. Note that each one is denoted by a letter.

N is the set of **natural numbers**, i.e. $\{1, 2, 3, \ldots\}$

> Remember the three dots signify the set goes on in the pattern shown forever, i.e. to infinity.

W is the set of **whole numbers**, i.e. $\{0, 1, 2, 3, \ldots\}$

Z is the set of **integers**, i.e. $\{\ldots, -3, -2, -1, 0, 1, 2, 3, \ldots\}$

this is also written as $\{0, \pm 1, \pm 2, \pm 3, \ldots\}$

Q is the set of **rational numbers**.

> A rational number is any number that can be represented by $\frac{p}{q}$ where p and q are both integers ($q \neq 0$).
>
> If we want p and q to belong to the set of integers we write $p, q \in \mathbf{Z}$. The symbol $\in$ means 'belongs to the set'.
>
> So $\frac{3}{2}, -\frac{7}{11}, 8$, etc., are rational numbers but $\sqrt{2}, \pi$, etc., are not!

R is the set of **real numbers**.

> The set of real numbers is the set of all possible numbers containing those listed previously and also those excluded such as $\sqrt{2}, \sqrt{3}, \pi$ etc.

Diagramatically these sets of numbers can be illustrated as

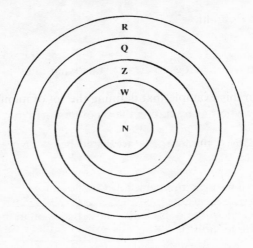

Symbol ⊂ means subset

Whole numbers **contain set of** natural numbers.

We say natural numbers are a **subset** of whole numbers, i.e.

natural numbers ⊂ whole numbers

N ⊂ W

Similarly

Integers contain whole numbers so contain natural numbers, i.e.

W ⊂ Z and N ⊂ Z

Rational numbers contain integers and so whole numbers and so natural numbers, i.e.

Z ⊂ Q and W ⊂ Q and N ⊂ Q

Every set of numbers is a subset of real numbers, i.e.

Q ⊂ R and Z ⊂ R and W ⊂ R and N ⊂ R

Worked Example 1.1

The solution of the equation $3x = 7$ when $x \in \mathbf{R}$ **is** $x = \dfrac{7}{3}$

However the equation $3x = 7$ when $x \in \mathbf{Z}$ has **no solution** since $\dfrac{7}{3}$ is not an integer.

You can see from this example that defining the set of numbers in use is very important.

In the above example, the solution set when $x \in \mathbf{R}$ is $\left\{\dfrac{7}{3}\right\}$ **but** the solution set when $x \in \mathbf{Z}$ is $\left\{\ \ \right\}$, i.e. the **empty set**, this can also be written as $\emptyset$.

1.1.2   BASIC CONCEPTS OF FUNCTIONS

Defining the set of numbers in use is vital when dealing with **functions**.

Definition If one quantity f is dependent upon another quantity x we say f is a function of x and write

$$f(x)$$

The set of possible values of x is called the **domain** of the function.

The set of possible related quantities is called the **range** of the function.

The following example illustrates this clearly.

Worked Example 1.2

Given the function $f(x) = x + 7, x \in \mathbf{Z}^+$ $\boxed{\text{or } \mathbf{N}}$. Note $\mathbf{Z}^+$ is the set of positive integers, i.e. $\{1, 2, 3, 4, \ldots\}$ this is $\mathbf{N}$.

The **domain** here is $\mathbf{Z}^+$ or $\mathbf{N}$.

However, the smallest possible value of $f(x) = 1 + 7 = 8$ and so the **range** is $f(x) \geqslant 8 \, f(x) \in \mathbf{Z}^+$ but we usually take $\mathbf{Z}^+$ or $\mathbf{N}$ to be the set. As it contains values not obtained by $f(x)$, i.e. 1 to 7, then it is called the **codomain** rather than range.

Functions are a very important aspect of mathematics and competence in their use and properties is essential for further study.

During your previous studies in mathematics you learned the basic properties of functions as demonstrated in the example on the following page.

Worked Example 1.3

(a) If $f(x) = 3x^2 - 2$ then $f(1) = 3(1^2) - 2$
$= 3 - 2 = 1$

using -3, then $f(-3) = 3(-3)^2 - 2$
$= 27 - 2 = 25$

using θ, then $f(\theta) = 3\theta^2 - 2$

(b) If $g(x) = \sin 2x°$ then $g(15) = \sin 30° = 0\cdot5$

and $g(30) = \sin 60° = \dfrac{\sqrt{3}}{2}$

Worked Example 1.4

(a) The function $f(t) = \sqrt{t}$ has domain $t \geqslant 0, t \in \mathbf{R}$, since $\sqrt{-ve}$ cannot be evaluated at this level of mathematics — however t can take **any** value greater than or equal to 0.

(b) The function $h(\theta) = \dfrac{\sin\theta}{\theta}$ has domain $\mathbf{R} - \{0\}$. Since you cannot divide by 0, θ can take any value whatsoever except 0.

1.1.3 COMPOSITE FUNCTIONS

A function of a function is called a **composite function**, examples of which are given below.

Worked Example 1.5

If $f(x) = 3x - 1$ and $g(x) = 2x + 3$, $x \in \mathbf{R}$, find the composite functions
(i) $f(g(x))$ and (ii) $g(f(x))$

Solution

(i) $f(g(x))$ | here $g(x) = 2x + 3$

$= f(2x + 3)$ | every time x is encountered in $f(x)$ replace it with $2x + 3$

$= 3(2x + 3) - 1$

$= 6x + 9 - 1$

$= 6x + 8$

(ii) $g(f(x))$ | here $f(x) = 3x - 1$ |

$= g(3x + 1)$ | every time x is encountered in $g(x)$ replace it with $3x + 1$ |

$= 2(3x + 1) + 3$

$= 6x + 2 + 3$

$= 6x + 5$

Note that $f(g(x)) \neq g(f(x))$ which is generally the case.

In some texts $f(g(x))$ is written as $(f{\circ}g)(x)$ or simply $(f{\circ}g)$ and $g(f(x))$ is written as $(g{\circ}f)(x)$ or simply $g{\circ}f$.

Worked Example 1.6

If $f(x) = \dfrac{1}{x}$, $x \neq 0$ and $g(x) = x$, $x \in \mathbf{R}$, find

(a) $f(f(x))$ (b) $g(g(x))$ (c) $f(g(x))$ (d) $g(f(x))$

Solution

(a) $f(f(x)) = f\left(\dfrac{1}{x}\right)$

$\qquad = \dfrac{1}{\frac{1}{x}} = x$

So here $f(f(x)) = g(x)$

(b) $g(g(x)) = g(x) = x$

in this case $g(g(x)) = g(x)$

(c) $f(g(x)) = f(x) = \dfrac{1}{x}$

and so $f(g(x)) = f(x)$

(d) $g(f(x)) = g\left(\dfrac{1}{x}\right) = \dfrac{1}{x} = f(x)$

here $g(f(x)) = f(x)$

Worked Example 1.7

(a) Given that $f(x) = \sin x$ and $g(x) = 2x$, $x \in \mathbf{R}$, find

    (a) $f(g(x))$ and   (b) $g(f(x))$

Solution

(a) $f(g(x)) = f(2x)$ $\boxed{\text{replace } x \text{ in } f(x) \text{ by } 2x.}$

        $= \sin 2x$

(b) $g(f(x)) = g(\sin x)$ $\boxed{\text{replace } x \text{ in } g(x) \text{ by } \sin x}$

        $= 2 \sin x$

Worked Example 1.8

If $f(x) = \sqrt{x}$, $x \geqslant 0$ and $g(x) = x^2 - 5$, $x \in \mathbf{R}$, find

(a) $f(g(3))$ and   (b) $g(f(3))$

Solution

(a) $f(g(3))$ $g(3) = 3^2 - 5 = 9 - 5 = 4$

    $= f(4)$

    $= \sqrt{4} = 2$

(b) $g(f(3))$ $f(3) = \sqrt{3}$

    $= g(\sqrt{3})$

    $= (\sqrt{3})^2 - 5$

    $= 3 - 5 = -2$

1.1.4   INVERSE OF A FUNCTION

In mathematics we often consider the case of 'undoing' some action.

To undo an addition we would subtract.

To undo a subtraction we would add.

So adding and subtracting are the **inverse** of each other.

To undo a multiplication we would divide.

To undo a division we would multiply.

So multiplication and division are the inverse of each other.

Similarly many functions have an **inverse**.

If some function $f(x)$ has an inverse we write
$$f^{-1}(x) \quad \text{or} \quad f^{-1}.$$

Worked Example 1.9

If $f(x) = 3x - 7$ find $f^{-1}(x)$.

Solution

$f(x) = 3x - 7$ | Step 1, let $y = f(x)$ |

$y = 3x - 7$

$3x = y + 7$ | Step 2, change subject of formula to x |

$x = \dfrac{1}{3}(y + 7)$

$\therefore f^{-1}(x) = \dfrac{1}{3}(x + 7)$ Inverse is now complete $x \rightarrow f^{-1}(x) \; y \rightarrow x$

Worked Example 1.10

If $g(x) = x^2 + 4, x \geqslant 0$ | If $x \in \mathbf{R}$ there would be **no** inverse since two
Find $g^{-1}(x)$ answers are possible from 1 value of x^2, e.g. $x^2 = 4, x \pm 2$ |

Solution

Let $g(x) = y$

$\qquad y = x^2 + 4$

$\Rightarrow \qquad x^2 = y - 4$

$\Rightarrow \qquad x = \sqrt{y - 4}$ | taking $+$ve square root |

$\therefore g^{-1}(x) = \sqrt{x - 4}$

Worked Example 1.11

Given that $g(x) = 4x + 3$ and $h(x) = \dfrac{1}{4}(x - 3), x \in \mathbf{R}$. Find

(a) $g(h(x))$ *(b)* $h(g(x))$ *(c)* Connection between g and h.

Solution

(a) $g(h(x)) = g\left(\frac{1}{4}(x-3)\right)$

$\qquad\qquad = 4\left(\frac{1}{4}(x-3)\right) + 3$

$\qquad\qquad = x - 3 + 3$

$\qquad\qquad = x$

(b) $h(g(x)) = h(4x + 3)$

$\qquad\qquad = \frac{1}{4}(4x + 3 - 3)$

$\qquad\qquad = \frac{1}{4} \times 4x$

$\qquad\qquad = x$

(c) They are the inverse of each other,

i.e. $g(x) = h^{-1}(x)$

$\qquad h(x) = g^{-1}(x)$

1.1.5   FUNCTIONS AND GRAPHS

Given the graph of any function $y = f(x)$, you should be able to draw the graph of an associated function such as $y = f(x) + a$ or $y = f(x + a)$.

The examples on the following pages illustrate these processes and you will find others throughout this book, in particular Sections 1.5.2 Exponential Functions, 1.5.3 Logarithmic Functions and 3.5.3 Phase Angles and other Graphs.

Worked Example 1.12

Given the graph of $y = f(x)$ below, draw the graph of

(a) $y = f(x) + 4$

(b) $y = f(x + 4)$

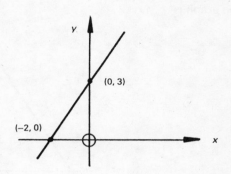

Solution

(a) The graph of $y = f(x) + 4$ is simply the graph of $f(x)$ 'moved up' 4 units vertically.

So $(0, 3) \rightarrow (0, 7)$

and $(-2, 0) \rightarrow (-2, 4)$

So graph is

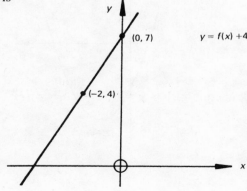

(b) The graph of $f(x + 4)$ is simply the graph of $f(x)$ 'moved' 4 units to the left horizontally.

So $(0, 3) \rightarrow (-4, 3)$

and $(-2, 0) \rightarrow (-6, 0)$

So graph is

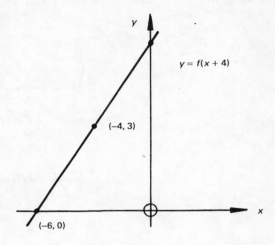

Worked Example 1.13

Given the graph of $y = g(x)$ below, sketch the graph of

(a) $y = g(x) - 3$

(b) $y = g(x - 3)$

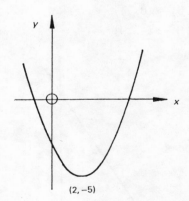

Solution

(a) Graph of $y = g(x) - 3$ is simply the graph of $y = g(x)$ 'moved' 3 units vertically downwards.

So $(2, -5) \rightarrow (2, -8)$

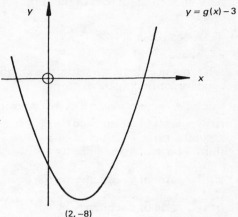

$y = g(x) - 3$

$(2, -8)$

(b) Graph of $y = g(x - 3)$ is simply the graph of $y = g(x)$ 'moved' 3 units horizontally to the right.

So $(2, -5) \rightarrow (5, -5)$

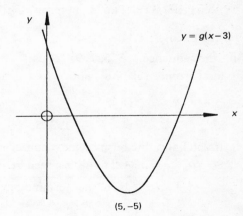

$y = g(x - 3)$

$(5, -5)$

Thus in general the graph of

(i) $y = f(x) + a$ is the graph of $y = f(x)$ moved a units vertically upwards if $a > 0$, **or** moved a units vertically downwards if $a < 0$.

(ii) $y = f(x + a)$ is the graph of $y = f(x)$ moved a units horizontally left when $a > 0$, **or** moved a units horizontally right when $a < 0$.

15

1.2 SEQUENCES

1.2.1 RECURRENCE RELATIONS

We have all seen sequences of the form

(a) $1, 3, 5, 7, 9, \ldots$

(b) $4, 12, 36, 108, \ldots$

(c) $-1, 1, 3, 5, 7, \ldots$

In each sequence there is a pattern and subsequent **terms** of the sequence can be found by continuing the pattern.

Each number in a sequence is called a **term** and it is usual to denote the

first   term of a sequence by u_1
second term of a sequence by u_2
third   term of a sequence by u_3
$\vdots$
tenth   term of a sequence by u_{10}
$\vdots$
nth   term of a sequency by u_n

Each of the above sequences can be defined in two ways

1.   As a recurrence relation, i.e. u_{n+1} in terms of u_n.

2.   As a general rule, i.e. u_n in terms of n.

Worked Example 1.14

Give the sequence $1, 3, 5, 7, 9, \ldots$ as

(a) a recurrence relation   and   *(b)* a general rule.

Solution

$$1, 3, 5, 7, 9, \ldots$$

(a) If you know one term the next consecutive term is found by **adding on 2**.

So $u_{n+1} = u_n + 2$ this is a **recurrence relation**.

> Note that terminology used is important
> $$u_{n-1}, \quad u_n, \quad u_{n+1}$$
> previous term $\leftarrow$ $\uparrow$ $\rightarrow$ next term
> nth term

You **must know** the nth term in order to find the $(n + 1)$th term with a recurrence relation.

(b) To find the general rule we have to compare the terms of the sequence with the set **N**.

Term No.   1   2   3   4   5   . . . n . . .
Term   1   3   5   7   9   . . .   ?   . . .

Since each term is **2 more** than previous term multiply term number by 2.

Term No. $\times$ 2   2   4   6   8   10   . . . $2n$ . . .

Compare these numbers **with terms** — difference in each case is 1.

Term No. $\times$ 2 – 1   1   3   5   7   9   . . . $2n-1$ . . .

$\therefore$ General rule is $u_n = 2n - 1$

This can be used to find any term of the sequence without having to know any of the other terms.

Worked Example 1.15

For the sequence 4, 12, 36, 108, . . ., find

(a) a recurrence relation   and   (b) a general rule which defines it.

Solution

4, 12, 36, 108, . . .

(a) If you know one term the next consecutive term is found by **multiplying by 3**.

So the recurrence relation is $u_{n+1} = 3u_n$

(b) Again to find the general rule we have to compare the terms of this sequence with the set **N**

Term No.   1   2   3   4   . . . n . . .
Term   4   12   36   108   . . .   ?   . . .

Here it is not so clear since terms are not increasing by a **constant amount**: and it is obvious that it is going to be a difficult task to find a general term — in this case defining the sequence by a recurrence relation is best!

The rule here is given by

$$4 = 12 \times \frac{1}{3} = 12 \times 3^{-1}$$

$u_n = 3^{n-1} \times 12$ since
$$\begin{aligned} 12 &= 12 \times 1 = 12 \times 3^0 \\ 36 &= 12 \times 3 = 12 \times 3^1 \\ 108 &= 12 \times 9 = 12 \times 3^2 \end{aligned}$$

Worked Example 1.16

Given the recurrence relation $u_{n+1} = u_n + 7$

find u_1, u_2, u_3 when $u_0 = 2$

Solution

If u_{n+1} $= u_0 + 7$

u_0 $= 2$

u_1 $= u_0 + 7 = \ 2 + 7 = 9$

u_2 $= u_1 + 7 = \ 9 + 7 = 16$

u_3 $= u_2 + 7 = 16 + 7 = 23$

(Sequence is 2, 9, 16, 23, ...)

Worked Example 1.17

A sequence is defined by the recurrence relation $u_{n+1} = \frac{1}{2}u_n$

Find u_1, u_2, u_3 and u_4 when $u_0 = 16$

Solution

If $u_{n+1} = \frac{1}{2}u_n$

u_0 $= 16$

u_1 $= \frac{1}{2}u_0 = \frac{1}{2} \times 16 = 8$

u_2 $= \frac{1}{2}u_1 = \frac{1}{2} \times \ 8 = 4$

u_3 $= \frac{1}{2}u_2 = \frac{1}{2} \times \ 4 = 2$

u_4 $= \frac{1}{2}u_3 = \frac{1}{2} \times \ 2 = 1$

$\therefore$ Sequence is 16, 8, 4, 2, 1, . . .

Examples 1.16 and 1.17 are both examples of special sequences.

An **arithmetic sequence** has a recurrence relation of the form

$$u_{n+1} = u_n + d$$

where d is a **constant**.

In example 1.16 d is 7.

A **geometric sequence** has a recurrence relation of the form
$$u_{n+1} = ru_n$$
where r is a **constant**.

In example 1.17 r is $\frac{1}{2}$.

In many problems we want to find out what the 'long term' effect is of a sequence.

Mathematically we write, 'what happens when $n \to \infty$', i.e. as n tends to infinity.

For an arithmetic sequence as $n \to \infty$ the terms are getting larger and larger if $d > 0$, i.e. $u_n \to \infty$ as $n \to \infty$.

If $d < 0$ then $u_n \to -\infty$ as $n \to \infty$.

The sequence is said to diverge.

For a geometric sequence as $n \to \infty$ then u_n is divergent if $r > 1$ or $r < -1$, however if $-1 < r < 1$ the sequence **converges**, i.e. **tends** to a given value.

This is clearly shown in the following examples.

Worked Example 1.18

If a sequence is defined by the recurrence relation $u_{n+1} = u_n + 3$

Find u_1, u_2, u_3 and u_4 if $u_0 = 3$ and find a formula for u_n. What happens to u_n as $n \to \infty$?

Solution

$u_{n+1} = u_n + 3$

$u_0 \quad = 3$

$u_1 \quad = u_0 + 3 = \quad 3 + 3 = 6$

$u_2 \quad = u_1 + 3 = \quad 6 + 3 = 9$

$u_3 \quad = u_2 + 3 = \quad 9 + 3 = 12$

$u_4 \quad = u_3 + 3 = 12 + 3 = 15$

$\therefore$ Sequence is 3, 6, 9, 12, 15, . . .

To find u_n we need to compare terms with **N**.

Term No.	1	2	3	4	5	. . .	n	. . .
Term		6	9	12	15	18	. . .	$3(n+1)$	. . .

Terms are increasing by 3 so try $3 \times$ term no.

$3 \times$ Term No.   6 9 12 15 $\ldots$ $3(n + 1)$ $\ldots$
These match term numbers so
$$u_n = 3(n + 1)$$
as $n \to \infty$, $u_n \to \infty$
i.e. the terms are getting bigger and bigger — obvious!

Worked Example 1.19

A sequence defined by the recurrence relation
$$u_{n+1} = \frac{1}{5} u_n$$
has $u_0 = 25$

(a) Find u_1, u_2, u_3 and u_4 and write down the sequence.

(b) Determine a formula for u_n.

(c) What happens to u_n as $n \to \infty$?

Solution

(a) $u_{n+1} = \frac{1}{5} u_n$

$u_0 \quad = 25$

$u_1 \quad = \frac{1}{5} u_0 = \frac{1}{5} \times 25 = 5$

$u_2 \quad = \frac{1}{5} u_1 = \frac{1}{5} \times \ 5 = 1$

$u_3 \quad = \frac{1}{5} u_2 = \frac{1}{5} \times \ 1 = \frac{1}{5}$

$u_4 \quad = \frac{1}{5} u_3 = \frac{1}{5} \times \ \frac{1}{5} = \frac{1}{25}$

Sequence is $25, 5, 1, \frac{1}{5}, \frac{1}{25}, \ldots$

(b) Note that $5 = 5^1$ term 1

$\qquad\qquad\quad 1 = 5^0$ term 2

$\qquad\qquad\quad \frac{1}{5} = 5^{-1}$ term 3

$\qquad\qquad\quad \frac{1}{25} = \frac{1}{5^2} = 5^{-2}$ term 4

$\therefore u_n = 5^{2-n}$

(c) As $n \to \infty$, $u_n \to 0$

$$\boxed{\begin{array}{l} \text{As } 3 - n \to -\infty \text{ as } n \to \infty \\ 5^{-\infty} = \dfrac{1}{5^{\infty}} = \dfrac{1}{\infty} = 0 \end{array}}$$

Worked Example 1.20

A sequence defined by the recurrence relation

$$u_{n+1} = 3u_n$$

has $u_0 = 1$.

(a) Find the first five terms of the sequence.

(b) Determine a formula for u_n.

(c) What happens to u_n as $n \to \infty$?

Solution

(a) $u_{n+1} = 3u_n$

$\quad u_0 \quad = 1$

$\quad u_1 \quad = 3 \times u_0 = 3 \times \ 1 = 3$

$\quad u_2 \quad = 3 \times u_1 = 3 \times \ 3 = 9$

$\quad u_3 \quad = 3 \times u_2 = 3 \times \ 9 = 27$

$\quad u_4 \quad = 3 \times u_3 = 3 \times 27 = 81$

$\quad \therefore$ Sequence is $1, 3, 9, 27, 81, \ldots$

(b) Note that we have **powers of 3**.

$\qquad 3 = 3^1 \quad$ term 1

$\qquad 9 = 3^2 \quad$ term 2

$\qquad 27 = 3^3 \quad$ term 3, etc

$\qquad \therefore u_n = 3^n$

(c) As $n \to \infty$, $u_n \to \infty$

$$\boxed{\begin{array}{l} \text{As } n - 1 \to \infty \\ \text{as } n \quad\ \ \to \infty \\ \qquad\quad 3^{\infty} \to \infty \end{array}}$$

In general we are interested in **linear recurrence relations** which are of the form

$$u_{n+1} = au_n + b$$

All the examples we have looked at have been of this form — although special cases have been noted.

When $a = 1$, i.e. $u_{n+1} = u_n + b$, we have an arithmetic sequence.

When $b = 0$, i.e. $u_{n+1} = au_n$, we have a geometric sequence.

Worked Example 1.21

For each of the recurrence relations find the first 5 terms.

(a) $u_{n+1} = 3u_n - 4 \qquad u_0 = 3$

(b) $u_{n+1} = 5 - 2u_n \qquad u_0 = 5$

Solution

(a) $u_{n+1} = 3u_n - 4$

$u_0 \quad = 3$

$u_1 \quad = 3 \times u_0 - 4 = (3 \times \ 3) - 4 = \ 9 - 4 = 5$

$u_2 \quad = 3 \times u_1 - 4 = (3 \times \ 5) - 4 = 15 - 4 = 11$

$u_3 \quad = 3 \times u_2 - 4 = (3 \times 11) - 4 = 33 - 4 = 29$

$u_4 \quad = 3 \times u_3 - 4 = (3 \times 29) - 4 = 87 - 4 = 83$

$\therefore$ Sequence is $3, 5, 11, 29, 83, \ldots$

(b) $u_{n+1} = 5 - 2u_n$

$u_0 \quad = 5$

$u_1 \quad = 5 - 2 \times u_0 = 5 - (2 \times 5) = 5 - 10 = -5$

$u_2 \quad = 5 - 2 \times u_1 = 5 - (2 \times (-5)) = 5 + 10 = 15$

$u_3 \quad = 5 - 2 \times u_2 = 5 - (2 \times 15) = 5 - 30 = -25$

$u_4 \quad = 5 - 2 \times u_3 = 5 - (2 \times (-25)) = 5 + 50 = 55$

$\therefore$ Sequence is $5, -5, 15, -25, 55, \ldots$

1.2.2   SERIES

A series is formed by adding together the terms of a sequence.

So for a general sequence

$$u_1, u_2, u_3, u_4, \ldots, u_n, \ldots$$

the corresponding series is given by

$$u_1 + u_2 + u_3 + u_4 + \ldots + u_n + \ldots$$

Here $S_1 = u_1$, i.e. sum of one term

$S_2 = u_1 + u_2$, i.e. sum of first two terms.

$S_3 = u_1 + u_2 + u_3$

$S_n = u_1 + u_2 + u_3 + \ldots + u_n$

From this we can see that

$S_2 - S_1 = (u_1 + u_2) - u_1 = u_1 - u_1 + u_2 = u_2$

$S_3 - S_2 = u_1 + u_2 + u_3 - (u_1 + u_2)$

$\qquad = u_1 - u_1 + u_2 - u_2 + u_3 = u_3$

and in general write

$S_n - S_{n-1} = u_n$

In many of the problems found in the Revised Higher examination, you will find the following useful. (Not in the syllabus but can be of great use!)

Geometric Series

We have already met geometric sequences (multiplying each term of a sequence by a constant to get the next term).

The recurrence relation was given by $u_{n+1} = ru_n$.

If we let a be the first term of a geometric sequence and the constant be r (called the **common ratio**), then the sequence can be defined by

$$a \quad , \quad ar \quad , \quad ar^2 \quad , \quad ar^3, \ldots, ar^{n-1}, \ldots$$

$\qquad\uparrow \qquad\qquad \uparrow \qquad\qquad \uparrow \qquad\qquad\qquad \uparrow$

$\qquad$ 1st term $\quad$ 2nd term $\quad$ 3rd term $\qquad\qquad$ nth term

i.e. $u_0 = a \qquad u_1 = ru_0 \qquad u_2 = r \times u_1$

$\qquad\qquad\qquad\qquad = ar \qquad\qquad = r \times ar$

$\qquad\qquad\qquad\qquad\qquad\qquad\qquad\quad = ar^2$

From this it is obvious that

$$S_n = a + ar + ar^2 + ar^3 + \ldots + ar^{n-1} \underline{\quad\quad} \text{①}$$

multiply both sides by r

$rS_n = ar + ar^2 + ar^3 + \ldots + ar^{n-1} + ar^n \underline{\quad\quad} \text{②}$

① $-$ ② $\ S_n - rS_n = a - ar^n$

$\Rightarrow (1 - r)S_n = a(1 - r^n)$

$\Rightarrow \qquad S_n = \dfrac{a(1 - r_n)}{1 - r} \quad \boxed{\text{This is the general form for } S_n}$

What happens to S_n as $n \to \infty$?

In $S_n = \dfrac{a(1-r^n)}{1-r}$ a and r are constants. The important term is r^n.

Let's investigate.

When $r > 1$. What happens to r^n as $n \to \infty$?

Let $r = 2$. $2^1 = 2, 2^2 = 4, 2^3 = 8, 2^4 = 16$, etc.

         As n gets bigger 2^n gets bigger, i.e. $n \to \infty \; 2^n \to \infty$

         This is true for all $r > 1$

         $\therefore$ as $n \to \infty \; r^n \to \infty$

When $r < -1$. What happens to r^n as $n \to \infty$?

Let $r = -2$. $(-2)^1 = -2, (-2)^2 = -4, (-2)^3 = -8, (-2)^4 = -16$, etc.

         As n gets bigger $(-2)^n$ oscillates between $+$ and $-$, i.e. $n \to \infty$,
         $(-2)^n \to \infty$ or $-\infty$

         This is true for all $r < -1$

When $-1 < r < 1$. What happens to r^n as $n \to \infty$?

Let $r = \dfrac{1}{2}$. $\dfrac{1}{2}^1 = \dfrac{1}{2}, \left(\dfrac{1}{2}\right)^2 = \dfrac{1}{2^2} = \dfrac{1}{4}, \left(\dfrac{1}{2}\right)^3 = \dfrac{1}{2^3} = \dfrac{1}{8}$

         As n gets bigger $\left(\dfrac{1}{2}\right)^2 \to 0$, i.e. $n \to \infty$, $\left(\dfrac{1}{2}\right)^2 \to 0$

Similarly

Let $r = -\dfrac{1}{2}$. $\left(-\dfrac{1}{2}\right)^1 = -\dfrac{1}{2}$ $\left(-\dfrac{1}{2}\right)^2 = \dfrac{1}{2^2} = \dfrac{1}{4}$ $\left(-\dfrac{1}{2}\right)^3 = -\dfrac{1}{8}$

         As n gets bigger $\left(-\dfrac{1}{2}\right)^n \to 0$, i.e. $n \to \infty$, $\left(-\dfrac{1}{2}\right)^n \to 0$

> This is true for **all** $-1 < r < 1$
> as $n \to \infty$, $r^n \to 0$

This is a very important result since given

$$S_n = \frac{a(1-r^n)}{1-r} \text{ when } -1 < r < 1$$

then $S_\infty = \dfrac{a(1-0)}{1-r}$ $r^n \to 0$ as $n \to \infty$

     $= \dfrac{a}{1-r}$

This describes the 'long term' effect on a geometric series.

Worked Example 1.22

Find the long term effect, i.e. as $n \to \infty$ of the following series.

(a) $1 + \frac{1}{2} + \frac{1}{4} + \frac{1}{8} + \frac{1}{16} + \ldots$

(b) $3 + 1 + \frac{1}{3} + \frac{1}{9} + \frac{1}{27} + \ldots$

(c) $25 - 5 + 1 - \frac{1}{5} + \frac{1}{25} + \ldots$

Solution

(a) $\quad 1 + \frac{1}{2} + \frac{1}{4} + \frac{1}{8} + \frac{1}{16} + \ldots$

$\quad = 1 + \frac{1}{2} + \frac{1}{2^2} + \frac{1}{2^3} + \frac{1}{2^4} + \ldots$

This is a geometric series with first term $a = 1$ and $r = \frac{1}{2}$.

$\quad \therefore$ as $n \to \infty \quad S_n = \frac{a}{1-r} = \frac{1}{1-\frac{1}{2}} = \frac{1}{\frac{1}{2}} = 2$

$\quad \therefore$ as $n \to \infty \quad 1 + \frac{1}{2} + \frac{1}{4} + \frac{1}{8} + \frac{1}{16} + \ldots \to 2$

(b) $\quad 3 + 1 + \frac{1}{3} + \frac{1}{9} + \frac{1}{27} + \ldots$

$\quad = 3 + 1 + \frac{1}{3} + \frac{1}{3^2} + \frac{1}{3^3} + \ldots$

This is a geometric series with first term $a = 3$ and $r = \frac{1}{3}$

$\quad \therefore$ as $n \to \infty \quad S_2 = \frac{a}{1-r} = \frac{3}{1-\frac{1}{3}} = \frac{3}{\frac{2}{3}} = \frac{9}{2}$

$\quad \therefore$ as $n \to \infty, \; 3 + 1 + \frac{1}{3} + \frac{1}{9} + \frac{1}{27} \to \frac{9}{2}$

(c) $\quad 25 - 5 + 1 - \frac{1}{5} + \frac{1}{25} + \ldots$

$\quad = 25 - 5 + 1 - \frac{1}{5} + \left(\frac{1}{5}\right)^2 + \ldots$

This is a geometric series with first term $a = 25$ and $r = -\frac{1}{5}$.

$$\therefore \text{ as } n \to \infty \quad S_n = \frac{a}{1-r} = \frac{25}{1-\left(-\frac{1}{5}\right)} = \frac{25}{1+\frac{1}{5}} = \frac{25}{\frac{6}{5}} = \frac{125}{6}$$

$$\therefore \text{ as } n \to \infty \quad 25 - 5 + 1 - \frac{1}{5} + \frac{1}{25} + \ldots \to \frac{125}{6}$$

You will find this technique invaluable as seen in the next section.

1.2.3   APPLICATIONS

Many of the problems asked in the Revised Higher examination have a real life slant as demonstrated in the following examples.

Worked Example 1.23

During a water cleaning process, 80% of pollutants are removed during each clean.

If no more pollutants are added between cleans, what percentage of pollutant remains after 5 cleans?

Solution

This is a simple recurrence relation

$$U_{n+1} = 0 \cdot 2 \, U_n \text{ where } U_{n+1} \text{ is the amount of pollutant left.}$$

Method I

Using $U_{n+1} = 0 \cdot 2 \, U_n$ where $U_0 = 1$

1st clean $U_1 = 0 \cdot 2 \times 1 = 0 \cdot 2$
2nd clean $U_2 = 0 \cdot 2 \times 0 \cdot 2 = 0 \cdot 04$
3rd clean $U_3 = 0 \cdot 2 \times 0 \cdot 04 = 0 \cdot 008$
4th clean $U_4 = 0 \cdot 2 \times 0 \cdot 008 = 0 \cdot 0016$
5th clean $U_5 = 0 \cdot 2 \times 0 \cdot 0016 = 0 \cdot 00032$

$\therefore 0 \cdot 032\%$ pollutant left

Method II

Using $U_n = 0 \cdot 2^n \, U_0 \qquad U_0 = 1$
$\qquad\qquad U_n = 0 \cdot 2^n$ where $n = $ number of cleans
$\qquad\qquad U_5 = 0 \cdot 2^5 = 0 \cdot 00032$

$\therefore 0 \cdot 032\%$ left.

Worked Example 1.24

Under certain lab conditions the height of a plant is given by

$$\text{height} = 0 \cdot 4\,[2 - (0 \cdot 75)^n]$$

where n = number of weeks after plant was first measured. Height is measured in cm.

(a) What was the height of the plant when it was first measured?

(b) How much did the plant grow at the start of the second week?

(c) Will the plant reach a height of 1 cm? Explain your answer.

Solution

(a) When first measured $n = 0$

$$\therefore \text{height} = 0 \cdot 4[2 - (0 \cdot 75)^0]$$
$$= 0 \cdot 4[2 - 1]$$
$$= 0 \cdot 4 \times 1$$
$$= 0 \cdot 4 \text{ cm}$$

$$\boxed{x^0 = 1}$$

(b) After 1 week, $n = 1$

$$\therefore \text{height} = 0 \cdot 4[2 - (0 \cdot 75)^1]$$
$$= 0 \cdot 4(2 - 0 \cdot 75)$$
$$= 0 \cdot 4 \times 1 \cdot 25$$
$$= 0 \cdot 5 \text{ cm}$$

This is the height at the start of the second week and so the amount the plant has grown is

$$\text{height when } n = 1 - \text{height when } n = 0$$
$$= 0 \cdot 5 - 0 \cdot 4$$
$$= 0 \cdot 1 \text{ cm}$$

(c) As $n \to \infty$ $\quad$ $0 \cdot 75^n \to 0$

So $2 - 0 \cdot 75^n \to 2 - 0 = 2$ as $n \to \infty$

$$\therefore \text{as } n \to \infty \quad \text{height} = 0 \cdot 4[2 - 0]$$
$$= 0 \cdot 4 \times 2$$
$$= 0 \cdot 8 \text{ cm}$$

Plant will not exceed $0 \cdot 8$ cm in height and so will not reach a height of 1 cm.

Worked Example 1.25

When testing a new drug it was found that it decays in the body at a rate of 20% during each 30 minute period after being administered.

(a) During hospital trials a patient is administered 200 units of the drug.

How much of the drug remains in the patient's bloodstream after four hours?

(b) If 200 units of this drug is administered every four hours and it is known that the drug is lethal should it exceed a level of 400 units, is this a safe dose for the patient?

Solution

(a) This situation can be modelled by the relation

> 20% decays leaves 80%, i.e. 0·8

$U_n = U_0 \times 0\cdot8^n$ where U_0 = initial dose (= 200)

$U_n = 200 \times 0\cdot8^n$ and n = no. of ½ hour periods

4 hours = 8 ½ hour periods

$n = 8$

After 4 hours $U_8 = 200 \times 0\cdot8^8$

$= 33\cdot55$

$= 34$ units of drug still remain

(b) Let U_n be recurrence relation modelled by this situation.

After   1st   four hours $U_1 = 200 \times 0\cdot8^8 + 200 = 200[1 + 0\cdot8^8]$

2nd four hours $U_2 = [200(1 + 0\cdot8^8)] \times 0\cdot8^8 + 200$

$= 200 [1 + 0\cdot8^8 + 0\cdot8^{16}]$

3rd four hours $U_3 = (200[1 + 0\cdot8^8 + 0\cdot8^{16}] \times 0\cdot8^8) + 200$

$= 200 [1 + 0\cdot8^8 + 0\cdot8^{16} + 0\cdot8^{24}]$

this continues so that

$$U_n = 200[1 + 0\cdot8^8 + 0\cdot8^{16} + 0\cdot8^{24} + \ldots + 0.8^{8n}]$$

as $n \to \infty$ what happens to $1 + 0\cdot8^8 + 0\cdot8^{16} + \ldots + 0\cdot8^{8n}$?

Using $S_\infty = \dfrac{a}{1-r}$ where $a = 1, r = 0\cdot8^8$

$$S_\infty = \frac{1}{1 - 0\cdot8^8} = 1\cdot2$$

$\therefore$ as $n \to \infty$ $U_n \to 200 \times 1\cdot2 = 240$

Dose that remains in body **does not** exceed 240 units and so dose is safe for patient.

1.3 QUADRATIC FUNCTION AND EQUATION

1.3.1 REVISION

Any expression of the form

$$ax^2 + bx + c \qquad a \neq 0, \quad a, b, c \in \mathbf{R}$$

is called a **quadratic expression**.

The associated equation $y = ax^2 + bx + c$ has a graph called a **parabola**,

which has shape 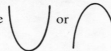 or

If $a > 0$ the parabola has shape

Such a parabola has a minimum turning point and so the quadratic has a minimum value.

If $a < 0$ the parabola has shape

Such a parabola has a maximum turning point and so the quadratic has a maximum value.

The point(s) where a parabola cuts the x-axis are called the **roots** or **zeroes** of the quadratic.

Any quadratic has at most 2 roots.

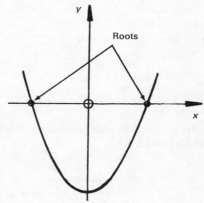

Roots

To determine the roots of any quadratic, the equation
$$ax^2 + bx + c = 0$$
must be solved.

29

There are two main methods of doing this

I Factorisation
II Quadratic Formula

Worked Example 1.26

Solve, by factorisation, the following quadratic equations.

(a) $x^2 + 7x + 6 = 0$ (b) $x^2 - 4x - 21 = 0$
(c) $2x^2 - 5x - 3 = 0$ (d) $6x^2 - 13x + 6 = 0$

Solution

(a) $x^2 + 7x + 6 = 0$ Factorising
$\Rightarrow (x + 6)(x + 1) = 0$
$\Rightarrow x + 6 = 0 \text{ or } x + 1 = 0$ $ab = 0$
$\Rightarrow x = -6 \text{ or } -1$ either $a = 0$ or $b = 0$ or $a = b = 0$

(b) $x^2 - 4x - 21 = 0$
$\Rightarrow (x - 7)(x + 3) = 0$
$\Rightarrow x - 7 = 0 \text{ or } x + 3 = 0$
$\Rightarrow x = 7 \text{ or } -3$

(c) $2x^2 - 5x - 3 = 0$
$\Rightarrow (2x + 1)(x - 3) = 0$
$\Rightarrow 2x + 1 = 0 \text{ or } x - 3 = 0$
$\Rightarrow x = -\dfrac{1}{2} \text{ or } 3$

(d) $6x^2 - 13x + 6 = 0$
$\Rightarrow (3x - 2)(2x - 3) = 0$
$\Rightarrow 3x - 2 = 0 \text{ or } 2x - 3 = 0$
$\Rightarrow x = \dfrac{2}{3} \text{ or } \dfrac{3}{2}$

If a quadratic has two roots the corresponding parabola cuts the x-axis at **two distinct points**, i.e.

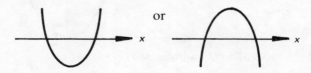

If a quadratic has one root only the corresponding parabola touches the *x*-axis at **one point only**, i.e.

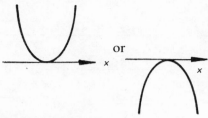

or

(The *x*-axis is a tangent to the parabola.)

If a quadratic has no roots the corresponding parabola **does not** touch or cross the *x*-axis.

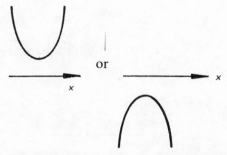

or

If a quadratic cannot be factorised then the quadratic formula will determine whether roots exist.

The quadratic formula is

$$x = \frac{-b \pm \sqrt{b^2 - 4ac}}{2a} \, , \, a \neq 0$$

Worked Example 1.27

Solve each of the following quadratic equations giving the roots correct to 1 decimal place.

(a) $x^2 - 4x - 11 = 0$ *(b)* $5 + 7x - 3x^2 = 0$

Solution

These quadratics cannot be factorised — hence use the quadratic formula.

(a) $x^2 - 4x - 11 = 0$

Compare $ax^2 + bx + c = 0$ here $a = 1$, $b = -4$, $c = -11$

$\therefore$ using quadratic formula

$$x = \frac{-b \pm \sqrt{b^2 - 4ac}}{2a} = \frac{-(-4) \pm \sqrt{(-4)^2 - 4.1.(-11)}}{2 \times 1}$$

$$= \frac{4 \pm \sqrt{16 + 44}}{2}$$

$$= \frac{4 \pm \sqrt{60}}{2} \quad \{\sqrt{60} = \sqrt{4 \times 15} = 2\sqrt{15}\}$$

$$= \frac{4 \pm 2\sqrt{15}}{2}$$

$$= 2 \pm \sqrt{15}$$

$$= 2 \pm 3\cdot873$$

$$= 5\cdot873 \text{ or } -1\cdot873$$

$$= 5\cdot9 \text{ or } -1\cdot9 \text{ (to 1 decimal place)}$$

(b) $5 + 7x - 3x^2 = 0$

Compare $ax^2 + bx + c = 0$ here $a = -3$, $b = 7$, $c = 5$

$$\boxed{\text{Be careful here!}}$$

$\therefore$ using quadratic formula

$$x = \frac{-b \pm \sqrt{b^2 - 4ac}}{2a} = \frac{-7 \pm \sqrt{7^2 - 4(-3)5}}{2 \times (-3)}$$

$$= \frac{-7 \pm \sqrt{49 + 60}}{-6}$$

$$= \frac{-7 \pm \sqrt{109}}{-6}$$

$$= \frac{-7 \pm 10\cdot440}{-6}$$

$$= \frac{3\cdot440}{-6} \text{ or } \frac{-17\cdot440}{-6}$$

$$= -0\cdot573 \text{ or } 2\cdot907$$

$$= -0\cdot6 \text{ or } 2\cdot9 \text{ (to 1 decimal place)}$$

1.3.2   COMPLETING THE SQUARE

Another method of solving quadratic equations is to **complete the square**.

Let us look at the method before solving any equations.

Worked Example 1.28

Complete the square with

(a) $x^2 + 4x - 7$

(b) $2x^2 - x + 8$

Solution

(a) $x^2 + 4x - 7$

$= (x^2 + 4x) - 7$

$= (x^2 + 4x + 4) - 7 - 4$

$= (x + 2)^2 - 11$

> We are interested in $x^2 + 4x$.
> To complete the square on $x^2 + 4x$ we require
> $x^2 + 4x + 4 = (x + 2)^2$

> added 4 so need to take away 4

So $x^2 + 4x - 7 = (x + 2)^2 - 11$ in completed square form.

> Note to complete the square with
>
> $$x^2 + ax$$
>
> half this value and square
>
> $$\therefore x^2 + ax + \left(\frac{a}{2}\right)^2 = \left(x + \frac{a}{2}\right)^2 \text{ or } \left(x^2 + ax + \frac{a^2}{4}\right)$$
>
> In above example $a = 4$ $\therefore \frac{a}{2} = \frac{4}{2} = 2$

(b) $2x^2 - x + 8$

$= 2\left(x^2 - \frac{1}{2}x\right) + 8$

$= 2\left(x^2 - \frac{1}{2}x + \left(\frac{1}{4}\right)^2\right) + 8$

$= 2\left(x - \frac{1}{4}\right)^2 + 8 - \frac{1}{8}$

$= 2\left(x - \frac{1}{4}\right)^2 + \frac{63}{8}$

> To complete the square the coefficient of
> x^2 **must be** 1

> Need to complete the square with $x^2 - \frac{1}{2}x$
>
> Here $a = \frac{1}{2}$ so $\frac{a}{2} = \frac{\frac{1}{2}}{2} = \frac{1}{4}$

> $2 \times \left(\frac{1}{4}\right)^2 = 2 \times \frac{1}{16} = \frac{1}{8}$ has been added

So $2x^2 - x + 8 = 2\left(x - \frac{1}{4}\right)^2 + \frac{63}{8}$ in completed square form.

Worked Example 1.29

Express $x^2 + 8x + 3$ in the form $(x + a)^2 + b$.

What is the minimum value of $x^2 + 8x + 3$?

Solution

$\quad x^2 + 8x + 3$ $\qquad$ | Completing the square |

$= (x^2 + 8x) + 3$

$= (x^2 + 8x + 16) + 3 - 16$ $\qquad$ | Here $a = 8$ so $\frac{a}{2} = 4$ |

$= (x + 4)^2 - 13$

$= (x + a)^2 + b$ $\qquad$ | $k^2 \geqslant$ for all values of k |

So $a = 4$ and $b = -13$

$\therefore (x + 4)^2 \geqslant 0$ so minimum value of $(x + 4)^2 = 0$

$\therefore$ minimum value of $x^2 + 8x + 3 = 0 - 13 = -13$

Alternate solution

Expand $(x + a)^2 + b$ and equate like terms!

$(x + a)^2 + b = x^2 + 2ax + a^2 + b$

$\qquad\qquad = x^2 + 8x + 3$

So $2a = 8 \Rrightarrow a = 4$

and $a^2 + b = 3 \Rrightarrow 4^2 + b = 3 \Rrightarrow b = 3 - 4^2$

$\qquad\qquad\qquad\qquad\qquad = 3 - 16$

$\qquad\qquad\qquad\qquad\qquad = -13$

$\therefore x^2 + 8x + 3 = (x + 4)^2 - 13$, etc.

Worked Example 1.30

Express $2 - 6x - x^2$ in the form $a - (x + b)^2$ and hence determine the maximum value of $2 - 6x - x^2$.

Solution

$$2 - 6x - x^2$$
$$= 2 - (6x + x^2)$$
$$= 2 - (x^2 + 6x)$$
$$= 2 - (x^2 + 6x + 9) + 9$$
$$= 11 - (x + 3)^2$$

So $a = 11$ and $b = 3$

completing the square on
$6x + x^2$ or $x^2 + 6x$
Here $a = 6 \Rightarrow \dfrac{a}{2} = 3$

'–' outside bracket makes
9 inside bracket a negative

Since $(x + 3)^2 \geqslant 0$

The maximum value occurs when $(x + 3)^2 = 0$

$\therefore$ maximum value of $2 - 6x - x^2 = 11 - 0$
$$= 11$$

Alternative Solution

Expand $a - (x + b)^2$ and equate like terms
$$a - (x + b)^2 = a - (x^2 + 2bx + b^2)$$
$$= a - b^2 - 2bx - x^2$$
$$= 2 - 6x - x^2$$

Here $2b = 6$
$\Rightarrow \quad b = 3$
and $a - b^2 = 2$
$\Rightarrow \quad a - 3^2 = 2$
$\Rightarrow \quad a - 9 \ = 2$
$\Rightarrow \quad a \qquad = 11$

1.3.3 DISCRIMINANT AND ITS PROPERTIES

The discriminant is given by

$$b^2 - 4ac$$

which is obtained from the quadratic formula

$$x = \frac{-b \pm \sqrt{b^2 - 4ac}}{2a}$$

The nature of the roots of any quadratic equation can be determined solely by examining the discriminant.

$b^2 - 4ac$ can only have 3 'states'.

$$b^2 - 4ac > 0 \Leftrightarrow \text{there are two real distinct roots}$$

The corresponding parabola cuts the x-axis at two different points.

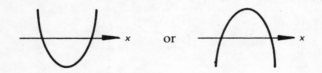

$$b^2 - 4ac = 0 \Leftrightarrow \text{there is one real root}$$
(some texts say a repeated root)

The corresponding parabola touches the x-axis at one point only.

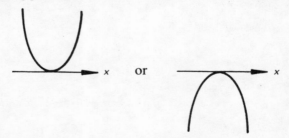

$$b^2 - 4ac < 0 \Leftrightarrow \text{there are no real roots.}$$

Note you cannot say there are no roots!

The corresponding parabola does not cut or touch the x-axis.

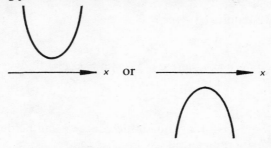

There are only real roots when $b^2 - 4ac \geqslant 0$

There are non-real roots when $b^2 - 4ac < 0$

Worked Example 1.31

For what value(s) of p does the quadratic equation $x^2 + px + 4 = 0$ have only one real root?

Solution

For one real root $b^2 - 4ac = 0$

From $x^2 + px + 4 = 0$

compare $ax^2 + bx + c = 0$ here $a = 1, b = p, c = 4$

and so $b^2 - 4ac$

$$= p^2 - 4(1)(4)$$

$$= p^2 - 16 = 0$$

$$\Rightarrow p^2 = 16$$

$$\Rightarrow p = \pm \sqrt{16} = \pm 4$$

Worked Example 1.32

Show that the roots of the equation

$$(k - 1)x^2 + kx + 1 = 0 \quad x \in \mathbf{R}$$

are always real.

Solution

For real roots we require $b^2 - 4ac \geqslant 0$

From $(k-1)x^2 + kx + 1 = 0$

compare $ax^2 + bx + c = 0$, here $a = k - 1, b = k, c = 1$

and so $\quad b^2 - 4ac$

$$= k^2 - 4(k-1)1$$
$$= k^2 - 4k + 4$$
$$= (k-2)^2$$

Since $(k-2)^2 \geqslant 0$ for all k

then $b^2 - 4ac \geqslant 0$

$\therefore$ roots are always real.

If a quadratic has two roots, the maximum/minimum value lies half-way between them.

If roots are x_1 and x_2 the minimum
value occurs when

$$x = \frac{x_1 + x_2}{2}$$

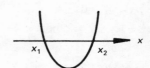

If roots are x_1 and x_2, the maximum
value occurs when

$$x = \frac{x_1 + x_2}{2}$$

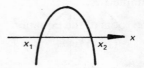

If a quadratic has only one root, the maximum/minimum value occurs at this root.

If root is x_1 the minimum value occurs at $x = x_1$
            the maximum value occurs at $x = x_1$

If a quadratic has no real roots, the maximum/minimum value can be found by completing the square.

1.3.4   QUADRATIC INEQUATIONS

From the graphs of $y = ax^2 + bx + c$,

| $ax^2 + bx + c > 0$ when the graph is **above** the x-axis. |

For example

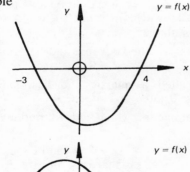

$f(x) > 0$
when
$x > 4$ or $x < -3$

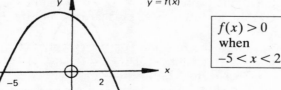

$f(x) > 0$
when
$-5 < x < 2$

$ax^2 + bx + c < 0$ when the graph is **below** the x-axis.

For example

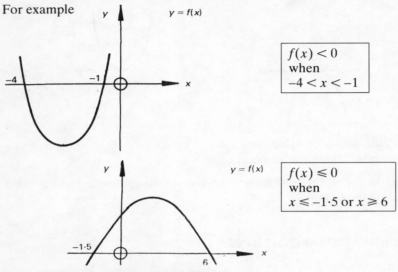

$f(x) < 0$
when
$-4 < x < -1$

$f(x) \leqslant 0$
when
$x \leqslant -1 \cdot 5$ or $x \geqslant 6$

1.4   REMAINDER THEOREM

1.4.1   REMAINDER THEOREM

From your previous studies in mathematics you should be able to **factorise** a quadratic expression quite easily. However it is not such an easy task to factorise a **polynomial** of degree 3 or above.

Note that a polynomial in degree 3 is called a **cubic** and has general form $ax^3 + bx^2 + cx + d$ where $a \neq 0$ and $a, b, c, d, e \in \mathbf{R}$

A polynomial in degree 4 is called a **quartic** and has general form $ax^4 + bx^3 + cx^2 + dx + e$ where $a \neq 0$ and $a, b, c, d, e \in \mathbf{R}$

Before proceeding further a few reminders, which you will find invaluable in this section, are given below.

Given the quadratic expression $x^2 - 3x - 4$, it can be factorised into $(x - 4)(x + 1)$. In this instance we say that $x - 4$ and $x + 1$ are **factors** of $x^2 - 3x - 4$.

Furthermore, given the function $f(x) = x^2 - 3x - 4$, if $x - 4$ is a factor then $x = 4$ is a solution of $f(x) = 0$, so $f(4) = 0$. Check it!
$f(4) = 4^2 - 3(4) - 4 = 16 - 12 - 4 = 0$

and similarly, if $x + 1$ is a factor then $x = -1$ is a solution of $f(x) = 0$ so $f(-1) = 0$, again check it!
$f(-1) = (-1)^2 - 3(-1) - (4) = 1 + 3 - 4 = 0$

This is in fact true for **any** polynomial.

In general we write

> If $x - a$ is a factor of any polynomial $f(x)$ then $f(a) = 0$

What if $x - a$ is not a factor of $f(x)$?

Let's see what happens!

Take the same example as above, i.e. $f(x) = x^2 - 3x - 4 = (x - 4)(x + 1)$.

We know $x - 2$ **is not** a factor of $f(x)$ and so $f(2)$, i.e. value of f when $x = 2$ should not be equal to 0

$\therefore f(2) = 2^2 - 3(2) - 4 = 4 - 6 - 4 = -6$

Think back to your early training in mathematics, there you learned that

$$4 \text{ is a factor of } 8 \text{ and so } 8 \div 4 \text{ or } \frac{8}{4} = 2 \text{ \textbf{with no} remainder.}$$

However,

$$3 \text{ is \textbf{not} a factor of } 8 \text{ and so } 8 \div 3 \text{ or } \frac{8}{3} = 2 \text{ with a remainder of 2.}$$

This is exactly what has happened above — since $x - 2$ is not a factor of $x^2 - 3x - 4$, the remainder is -6 when $x^2 - 3x - 4$ is divided by $x - 2$!

We are going to use these facts to help find the factors (if any) of cubics and quartics.

Worked Example 1.33

Factorise fully $x^3 - 2x^2 - 5x + 6$

Solution

To factorise this we are going to 'detach the coefficients' and use 'synthetic division'.

To do this make a table like that opposite.

| 1 | −2 | −5 | 6 |

  1 is the coefficient of the x^3 term.
−2 is the coefficient of the x^2 term.
−5 is the coefficient of the x term.
  6 is the constant term.

We do not know a factor and so have to 'guess' a factor. The most likely choices are ± 1, ± 2, ± 3, but you have to keep on trying numbers until you get a zero remainder.

> **Note:** A method called 'nested factorisation' is the quickest way to evaluate $x^3 - 2x^2 - 5x + 6$ on your calculator for any value of x.
>
> $$x^3 - 2x^2 - 5x + 6 = x(x^2 - 2x - 5) + 6$$
> $$= x[x(x - 2) - 5] + 6$$
>
> On your calculator evaluate
>
> $x - 2 \times x - 5 \times x + 6$
>
> for a given value of x.

When $x = 1$ $x^3 - 2x^2 - 5x + 6 = 0$

> On your calculator
> $-1 - 2 \times (-1) - 5 \times (-1) + 6$

and so $x - 1$ is a factor of the cubic.

To determine the other factors we now make use of the detached coefficients.

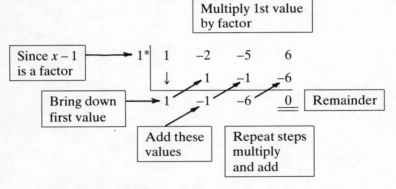

Since remainder is 0, then $x - 1$ is a factor and

$x^3 - 2x^2 - 5x + 6 = (x - 1)(x^2 - x - 6)$ These values are obtained from 1, -1 and -6 from above table

$x^2 - x - 6$ is a quadratic
which is easily factorised.

$\therefore x^3 - 2x^2 - 5x + 6 = (x - 1)(x - 3)(x + 2)$

Since $x - 3$ and $x + 2$ are also factors then 3 or -2 at * above would also have given a remainder of 0.

Since $x - 2$ is not a factor the remainder is not 0.

When $x = 2$ With detached coefficients
$$x^3 - 2x^2 - 5x + 6 = -4$$

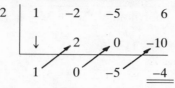

The remainder gives the same result!

However the 'detached coefficients' method gives us more information, from it we can state that

$$x^3 - 2x^2 - 5x + 6 = (x - 2)(x^2 + 0x - 5) - 4 \longleftarrow \boxed{\text{Remainder}}$$
$$= (x - 2)(x^2 - 5) - 4$$

This can be easily checked by expanding! Try it.

Worked Example 1.34

Factorise fully $x^3 - 3x - 2$

> As a nested polynomial, $x^3 - 3x - 2 = x(x^2 - 3) - 2$
> i.e. evaluate $x^2 - 3 \times x - 2$

Solution

When $x = 1$, $x^3 - 3x - 2 = -4$
When $x = -1$, $x^3 - 3x - 2 = 0$
Thus $x = -1$ gives a remainder of 0
and so $x + 1$ is a factor of $x^3 - 3x - 2$.

Using detached coefficients

> Although there is no x^2 term it must be shown with a **zero coefficient** in its proper place when using synthetic division.

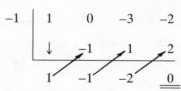

Since remainder is zero $x + 1$ is a factor and so

$$x^3 - 3x - 2 = (x + 1)(x^2 - x - 2)$$
$$= (x + 1)(x - 2)(x + 1)$$
$$= (x + 1)^2(x - 2)$$

43

Worked Example 1.35

Factorise fully $2x^3 + 3x^2 - 11x - 6$

> As a nested polynomial, $2x^3 + 3x^2 - 11x - 6$
> $= x(2x^2 + 3x - 11) - 6$
> $= x[x(2x + 3) - 11] - 6$
> i.e. evaluate $2x + 3 \times x - 11 \times x - 6$

Solution

The value of $2x^3 + 3x^2 - 11x - 6$

When $x = 1$ is -12, $x = -1$ is 6, $x = 2$ is 0

Thus $x = 2$ gives a remainder of 0

and so $x - 1$ is a factor of $2x^3 + 3x^2 - 11x - 6$

Detaching coefficients and using
synthetic division

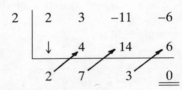

Since remainder is zero, $x - 2$ is a factor and so
$2x^3 + 3x^2 - 11x - 6 = (x - 2)(2x^2 + 7x + 3)$
$\qquad\qquad\qquad = (x - 2)(2x + 1)(x + 3)$

Worked Example 1.36

If $(x + 5)$ is a factor of $x^3 - 9x^2 + ax + 15$ find the value of a.

Solution

Since $x + 5$ is a factor then $x = -5$ will give a 'remainder' of 0

When $x = -5$, $x^3 + 9x^2 + ax + 15$
$\qquad\qquad = -125 + 225 - 5a + 15$
$\qquad\qquad = 115 - 5a$
$\qquad\qquad = 0$

So $\qquad 5a = 115$
$\qquad\quad a = \dfrac{115}{5} = 23$

Although detaching coefficients and using synthetic division would have worked here there was no need to as the cubic did not have to be fully factorised.

However, if $x^3 + 9x^2 + ax + 15$ with $(x + 5)$ as a factor had to be fully factorised the method below is easier.

Since $x + 5$ is a factor remainder **is** 0.

So $115 - 5a = 0$

$$5a = 115$$

$$a = 23$$

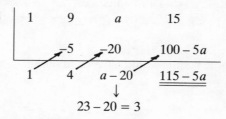

and thus $x^3 + 9x^2 + 23x + 15$

$$= (x + 5)(x^2 + 4x + 3)$$

$$= (x + 5)(x + 3)(x + 1)$$

Worked Example 1.37

If $(x - 2)$ and $(x + 3)$ are factors of $x^3 + px^2 + qx + 30$, find values of p and q.

Solution

Since there is **no need** to fully factorise the final cubic, synthetic division need not be used.

Since $x - 2$ is a factor then $x = 2$ will yield a value of 0.

$$\therefore 2^3 + p(2)^2 + q(2) + 30 = 0$$

$\Rightarrow \qquad 4p + 2q + 38 = 0$ $\boxed{\text{Common factor of 2}}$

$\Rightarrow \qquad 2(2p + q + 19) = 0$

$\Rightarrow \qquad 2p + q + 19 = 0 \ \text{———} \ ①$

Since $x + 3$ is a factor then $x = -3$ will yield a value of 0.

$$\therefore (-3)^3 + p(-3)^2 + q(-3) + 30 = 0$$

$\Rightarrow \qquad 9p - 3q + 3 = 0$ $\boxed{\text{Common factor of 3}}$

$\Rightarrow \qquad 3(3p - q + 1) = 0$

$\Rightarrow \qquad 3p - q + 1 = 0 \ \text{———} \ ②$

$\therefore$ Solving the simultaneous equations ① and ② will give values of p and q.

$$2p + q = -19 \quad\text{———}\quad ①$$
$$3p - q = -1 \quad\text{———}\quad ②$$

$① + ②$ $\quad 5p \quad\quad = -20$

$\quad\quad\quad\quad p \quad\quad = -4$

Substitute $p = -4$ into equation $①$

$$-8 + q = -19$$
$$\Rightarrow \quad q = -11$$

The same results would have been obtained with synthetic division.

When $x = 2$

$$
\begin{array}{c|cccc}
2 & 1 & p & q & 30 \\
  & \downarrow & 2 & 4 + 2p & 8 + 4p + 2q \\
\hline
  & 1 & 2 + p & 4 + 2p + q & 38 + 4p + 2q
\end{array}
$$

Since remainder **must be** 0 then

$$38 + 4p + 2q = 0 \qquad \boxed{\text{Common factor 2}}$$
$$\Rightarrow 2(19 + 2p + q) = 0$$
$$\Rightarrow \quad 19 + 2p + q = 0 \quad\text{———}\quad ①$$

Similarly,

when $x = -3$

$$
\begin{array}{c|cccc}
-3 & 1 & p & q & 30 \\
   & \downarrow & -3 & -3p + 9 & -3q + 9p - 27 \\
\hline
   & 1 & p - 3 & q - 3p + 9 & -3q + 9p + 3
\end{array}
$$

Again, since remainder must be 0 then

$$9p - 3q + 3 = 0 \qquad \boxed{\text{Common factor 3}}$$
$$\Rightarrow 3(3p - q + 1) = 0$$
$$\Rightarrow \quad 3p - q + 1 = 0 \quad\text{———}\quad ②$$

Now solving the simultaneous equations $①$ and $②$ (same as above) will yield $p = -4$ and $q = -11$

Worked Example 1.38

$(x - 1)$ is a factor of $f(x) = x^3 + ax^2 + bx - 9$ and when $f(x)$ is divided by $x - 2$ the remainder is 25.

Find the values of a and b and hence, or otherwise, factorise fully $f(x)$.

Since $f(x)$ is to be fully factorised then the best method to use is synthetic division.

Since $x - 1$ is a factor $x = 1$ will yield a remainder of 0

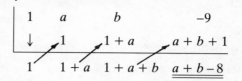

Remainder is 0

$\therefore a + b - 8 = 0$

$\Rightarrow a + b \quad = 8 \text{——} ①$

Since $x - 2$ yields a remainder of 25 then $x = 2$ yields remainder of 25

Remainder is 25

$4a + 2b - 1 = 25$

$\Rightarrow \quad 4a + 2b \ = 26$ | Common factor 2 |

$\Rightarrow 2(2a + b) = 26$

$\Rightarrow \quad 2a + b \ = 13 \text{——} ②$

Solving the simultaneous equations ① and ②

$$a + b = 8 \text{——} ①$$
$$2a + b = 13 \text{——} ②$$

$② - ① \qquad a = 5$

Substitute $a = 5$ into equation ①

$$5 + b = 8$$
$$b = 3$$

$\therefore f(x) = x^3 + 5x^2 + 3x - 9$

Returning to ** we have

and so

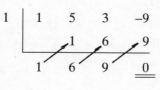

$f(x) = x^3 + 5x^2 + 3x - 9$

$\quad = (x - 1)(x^2 + 6x + 9)$

$\quad = (x - 1)(x + 3)^2$

47

Worked Example 1.39

Factorise fully $2x^4 + 7x^3 - 10x^2 - 33x + 18$.

Although a quartic the same process as the previous page applies.

Solution

We need to find **one** factor in order to proceed.

As a nested polynomial
$2x^4 + 7x^3 - 10x^2 - 33x + 18$
$= x(2x^3 + 7x^2 - 10x - 33) + 18$
$= x[x(2x^2 + 7x - 10) - 33] + 18$
$= x[x[x(2x + 7) - 10] - 33] + 18$
i.e. $2x + 7 \times x - 10 \times x - 33 \times x + 18$

The value of
$2x^4 + 7x^3 - 10x^2 - 33x + 18$
when $x = 1$ is
$\qquad x = -1$ is
$\qquad x = 2$ is 0
Thus $x = 2$ gives a remainder of 0
and so $(x - 2)$ is a factor of
$2x^4 + 7x^3 - 10x^2 - 33x + 18$

Using synthetic division

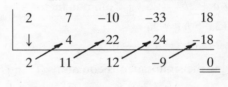

Thus

$2x^4 + 7x^3 - 10x^2 - 33x + 18$
$= (x - 2)(2x^3 + 11x^2 + 12x - 9)$

We have to repeat this process with $2x^3 + 11x^2 + 12x - 9$

when $x = 1$ its value is 16
$\qquad x = -1$ its value is -12
$\qquad x = 2$ its value is 75
$\qquad x = -2$ its value is -5
$\qquad x = 3$ its value is 180
$\qquad x = -3$ its value is 0

Thus $x = -3$ gives a remainder of 0.

and so $(x + 3)$ is a factor of $2x^3 + 11x^2 + 12x - 9$

Again using synthetic division

$$
\begin{array}{c|cccc}
-3 & 2 & 11 & 12 & -9 \\
 & \downarrow & -6 & -15 & 9 \\
\hline
 & 2 & 5 & -3 & 0
\end{array}
$$

Thus

$2x^3 + 11x^2 + 12x - 9$
$= (x + 3)(2x^2 + 5x - 3)$
$= (x + 3)(2x - 1)(x + 3)$
$= (x + 3)^2(2x - 1)$
$\therefore 2x^4 + 7x^3 - 10x^2 - 33x + 18 = (x - 2)(x + 3)^2(2x - 1)$

Worked Example 1.40

Show that $(2x - 1)$ is a factor of $2x^3 - 7x^2 - 17x + 10$ and hence factorise the expression fully.

Solution

If $2x - 1$ is a factor, $x = \dfrac{1}{2}$ will give a remainder of 0 with synthetic division.

Since remainder is 0 then

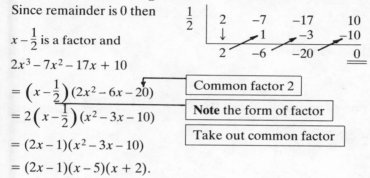

$x - \dfrac{1}{2}$ is a factor and

$2x^3 - 7x^2 - 17x + 10$

$= \left(x - \dfrac{1}{2}\right)(2x^2 - 6x - 20)$ Common factor 2

$= 2\left(x - \dfrac{1}{2}\right)(x^2 - 3x - 10)$ **Note** the form of factor

$= (2x - 1)(x^2 - 3x - 10)$ Take out common factor

$= (2x - 1)(x - 5)(x + 2).$

1.5   EXPONENTIAL AND LOGARITHMIC FUNCTION

1.5.1   REVISION OF INDICES

Both in this section and throughout your study of mathematics, the laws of indices, stated below, are of great use.

If m and $n \in \mathbf{Q}$ (i.e. m and n are rational numbers)

I $a^m \times a^n = a^{m+n}$

    e.g. $a^2 \times a^4 = a^{2+4} = a^6$

    Since $a^2 = a \times a$ and $a^4 = a \times a \times a \times a$

    So $a^2 \times a^4 = a \times a \times a \times a \times a \times a = a^6$

II $a^m \div a^n = \dfrac{a^m}{a^n} = a^{m-n}$ $(a \neq 0)$

    e.g. $a^5 \div a^2 = \dfrac{a^5}{a^2} = a^{5-2} = a^3$

    Since $a^5 = a \times a \times a \times a \times a$ and $a^2 = a \times a$

    So $\dfrac{a^5}{a^2} = \dfrac{\cancel{a} \times \cancel{a} \times a \times a \times a}{\cancel{a} \times \cancel{a}} = a \times a \times a = a^3$

III $(a^m)^n = a^{mn}$ **Be careful not to mix this up with rule I**

e.g. $(a^2)^3 = a^{2 \times 3} = a^6$

Since $a^2 = a \times a$

So $(a^2)^3 = (a \times a)^3 = (a \times a) \times (a \times a) \times (a \times a)$
$$= a \times a \times a \times a \times a \times a$$
$$= a^6$$

IV $a^0 = 1 \qquad a \neq 0$

$a^1 = a$

e.g. $105^0 = 1 \qquad -3^0 = 1$

V $\dfrac{1}{a^m} = a^{-m} \qquad a \neq 0$

This can be proved using rules II and IV

$$\frac{1}{a^m} = \frac{a^0}{a^m} = a^{0-m} = a^{-m}$$

VI $a^{1/m} = \sqrt[m]{a}$

e.g. $a^{1/2} = \sqrt{a} \qquad a^{1/3} = \sqrt[3]{a}$

VII $a^{m/n} = \sqrt[n]{a^m}$ or $(\sqrt[n]{a})^m$, $n \in \mathbf{Z}^+$

1.5.2 EXPONENTIAL FUNCTIONS

Any function of the form

$$f(x) = a^x \quad a > 0$$
$$a \neq 1$$

Note variable is the power or index or exponent

is called an **exponential function**

If $a = 1$, $f(x) = 1^x = 1$

Since $a > 0$ it can be shown that $f(x) > 0$ for all values of x.

When $a > 1$ the general form of
the graph $y = a^x$ is

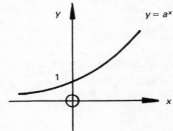

When $0 < a < 1$ the general form of the graph $y = a^x$ is

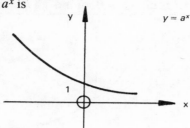

Worked Example 1.41

The graph opposite is that of $y = 3^x$

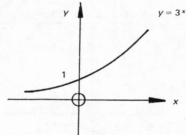

Sketch the graphs of

(a) $y = 3^{-x}$

(b) $y = 3^x + 2$

(c) $y = -3^x$

(d) $y = 2 - 3^x$

Solution

(a) Given the graph of $y = a^x$ the graph of $y = a^{-x}$ is simply the graph of $y = a^x$ reflected in y-axis.

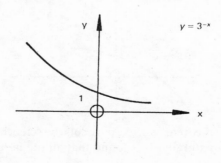

(b) | $y = a^x + k$ is the graph of
$y = a^x$ moved k places **up** if $k > 0$, or moved k places **down** if $k < 0$.

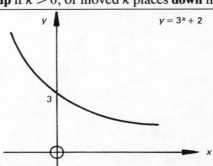

(c) | Graph of $y = -a^x$ is simply the graph of $y = a^x$ reflected in x-axis.

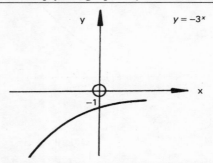

(d) | $y = 2 - 3^x = -3^x + 2$
This is the graph of $y = 3^x$ reflected in the x-axis and moved up 2 places.

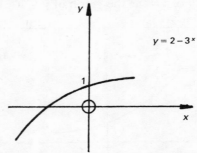

In many aspects of the real world, particularly science and engineering, things grow or decay naturally. It is found that all the natural laws of growth

and decay can be 'modelled' mathematically in an equation of the form
$$y = Ae^x$$
where e is a mathematical constant that is frequently used in mathematics,
$e = 2 \cdot 7183 \ldots$

A is also a constant.

The exponential function
$$f(x) = e^x \text{ or exp } (x)$$
is one of the most important mathematical functions that you will meet many times if you continue your studies in mathematics.

Section 1.5.4 shows some applications of this function.

The graphs of $y = e^x$ and $y = e^{-x}$ are shown below.

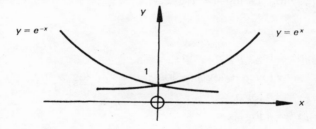

1.5.3 LOGARITHMIC FUNCTIONS

If $y = a^x$ the logarithmic function can be given as $x = \log_a y$, i.e. the logarithmic function is the **inverse** of the exponential function.

Worked Example 1.42

(a) $\log_2 8 = 3$ since $2^3 = 8$

(b) $\log_5 25 = 2$ since $5^2 = 25$

(c) $\log_{16} 4 = \dfrac{1}{2}$ since $16^{1/2} = 4$

Thus any function of the form
$$f(x) = \log_a x \quad x > 0$$
is called a **logarithmic function**.

53

a is called the **base** of the logarithm and the most frequently used bases are 10 and e.

Note that • $\log_{10}x$ is shown by log button on your calculator

  • $\log_e x$ is also written as $\ln x$ (called the natural logarithm).

There are a number of rules for logarithms that you must know.

I $\log_a pq = \log_a p + \log_a q$

e.g. $\log_{49}7a = \log_{49}7 + \log_{49} a = \dfrac{1}{2} + \log_{49}a$

II $\log_a \dfrac{p}{q} = \log_a p - \log_a q$

e.g. $\log_2 \dfrac{x}{4} = \log_2 x - \log_2 4 = \log_2 x - 2$

III $\log_a p^n = n \log_a p$

since $\log_a p^n = \log_a (\overset{\leftarrow\, n \text{ times} \,\rightarrow}{p\,p\,p \ldots p})$

$= \log_a p + \log_a p + \log_a p + \ldots + \log_a p$

$= n \log_a p$

e.g. $\log_{10}x^4 = 4 \log_{10}x$

IV $\log_a a = 1$

Since $a^1 = a$

e.g. $\log_5 5 = 1$

V $\log_a 1 = 0$

Since $a^0 = 1$

e.g. $\log_e 1 = 0$

The graph of $y = \log_a x$ is shown opposite and it is clear that x must be greater than or equal to 0.

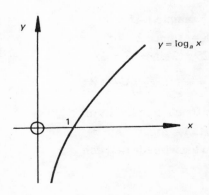

$y = \log_a x$

Worked Example 4.43

The graph opposite is that of
$$y = \log_5 x$$
Sketch the graphs of

(a) $y = \log_5 x + 2$

(b) $y = -\log_5 x$

(c) $y = \log_5(x - 3)$

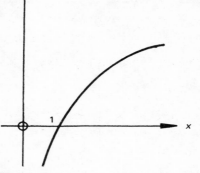

Solution

(a) Graph of $y = \log_5 x + 2$ is simply graph of $y = \log_5 x$ moved **up** 2 places.

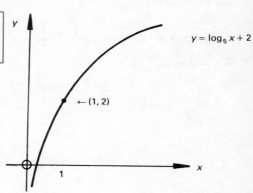

(b) Graph of $y = -\log_5 x$ is simply graph of $y = \log_5 x$ reflected in x-axis.

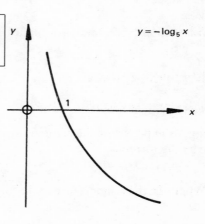

(c) | Graph of $y = \log_5(x - 3)$ is simply the graph of $y = \log_5 x$ moved 3 places to the **right**.

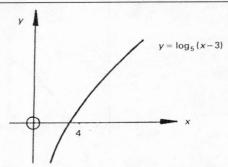

In particular the graphs of $y = e^x$ and $y = \log_e x$ are shown in the diagram below.

| The line $y = x$ is an axis of symmetry

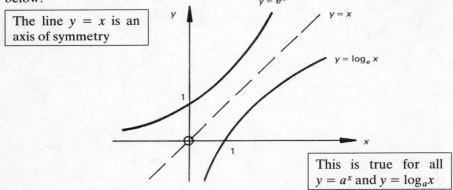

| This is true for all $y = a^x$ and $y = \log_a x$

As with section 1.5.2, there are applications of this function in section 1.5.4

1.5.4 APPLICATIONS

Worked Example 1.44

During an experiment the temperature (°C) of a solution after t minutes is given by the formula

$$C(t) = 50e^{-0.02t}$$

(a) What was the temperature at the start of the experiment?

(b) What was the temperature of the solution after 1 hour?

(c) How long did the solution take to reach a temperature of 10 °C? (Answer to the nearest minute.)

Solution

(a) At start of the experiment $t = 0$.

$\therefore C(0) = 50e^{-0.02 \times 0} = 50e^0 = 50 \times 1 = 50$

$\therefore$ temperature = 50 °C at start of the experiment.

(b) After 1 hour, $t = 60$ minutes

> Remember t is in minutes

$C(60) = 50e^{-0.02 \times 60}$

$= 50e^{-1.2}$ On your calculator use e^x button

$= 15.06$

$= 15.1$

$\therefore$ temperature is 15.1 °C (to 1 d.p.) after 1 hour.

(c) When temperature = 10 °C then $C(t) = 10$

$\therefore 10 = 50e^{-0.02t}$ $\dfrac{10}{50} = \dfrac{1}{5} = 0.2$

$\Rightarrow e^{-0.02t} = \dfrac{1}{5}$

$\Rightarrow e^{-0.02t} = 0.2$

taking $\log_e$ of both sides

> Need to find t
> Want to move e^{At} to $At = \ldots$
> To do this use logs
>
> $\log_e e = 1$
>
> $\log_e e^x = x \log_e e$
>
> $= x$

$\Rightarrow \log_e e^{-0.02t} = \log_e 0.2$

$\Rightarrow -0.02t \log_e e = \log_e 0.2$

$\Rightarrow \qquad -0.02t = \log_e 0.2$

$\Rightarrow \qquad t = \dfrac{\log_e 0.2}{-0.02}$ To calculate $\log_e 0.2$ use ln button on your calculator.

$= 80.47$

$\therefore$ time taken to reach temperature is 80 minutes to the nearest minute.

Worked Example 1.45

Explain how the graph of $y = \log_7 7x$ can be drawn given the graph of $y = \log_7 x$.

Solution

Using the rule $\log_a pq = \log_a p + \log_a q$

then $\log_7 7x = \log_7 7 + \log_7 x$

and $\log_a a = 1$

then $\log_7 7 = 1$

$\therefore y = \log_7 7x = \log_7 7 + \log_7 x$

$\qquad\qquad\quad = 1 + \log_7 x$

$\therefore$ graph of $y = \log_7 7x$ is the graph of $y = \log_7 x$ moved up **1 place**.

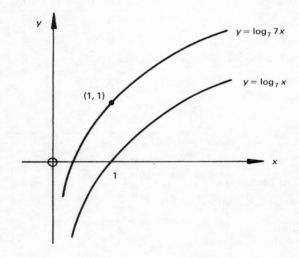

Similarly the graph of $y = \log_5 25x$ is the graph of $y = \log_5 x$ moved up 2 places, i.e. $y = \log_5 x + 2$

Since $\log_5 25x = \log_5 25 + \log_5 x$ $\qquad \log_5 25 = 2$

$\qquad\qquad\quad = 2 + \log_5 x$ $\qquad\qquad$ since $5^2 = 25$

Worked Example 1.46

The graph opposite illustrates the law

$$b = ka^n$$

What are the values of k and n?

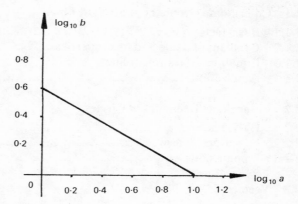

Solution

Graph is of a straight line and so must be of the form

$$y = mx + c$$

From the graph: y-intercept c is $0 \cdot 6$

and gradient m is $-\dfrac{0 \cdot 6}{1 \cdot 0} = -\dfrac{3}{5}$ or $-0 \cdot 6$

$\therefore$ equation of line is $y = -0 \cdot 6x + 0 \cdot 6$

> Need to transform $b = ka^n$ into the form $y = mx + c$.
> To do this take $\log_{10}$ of both sides.

$b = ka^n$

$\Leftrightarrow \log_{10}b = \log_{10}(ka^n)$

$\Leftrightarrow \log_{10}b = \log_{10}k + \log_{10}a^n$

$\Leftrightarrow \log_{10}b = \log_{10}k + n\log_{10}a$

$\Leftrightarrow \log_{10}b = n\log_{10}a + n\log_{10}k$

Compare $y = mx + c$

Here $m = n = -0 \cdot 6$

$c = \log_{10}k = 0 \cdot 6 \Leftrightarrow k = 10^{0 \cdot 6}$ or $3 \cdot 98$ (to 2 d.p.)

SECTION 2   CO-ORDINATE GEOMETRY

2.1 CO-ORDINATE GEOMETRY OF STRAIGHT LINES

2.1.1 BASIC FACTS

Distance Formula

The distance between **any** two points (x_1, y_1) and (x_2, y_2) is given by the **distance formula**

$$d = \sqrt{(x_2 - x_1)^2 + (y_2 - y_1)^2}$$

where d is the distance.

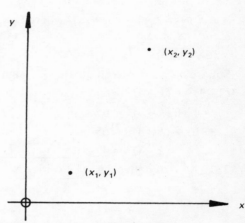

This can also be used to find the length of a line between two points.

Worked Example 2.1

Calculate the length of the line joining the points $(1, 5)$ and $(5, 8)$

Solution

Let length of line be l

$$
\begin{aligned}
l &= \sqrt{(x_2 - x_1)^2 + (y_2 - y_1)^2} \text{ where } \\
  &= \sqrt{(5 - 1)^2 + (8 - 5)^2} \\
  &= \sqrt{4^2 + 3^2} \\
  &= \sqrt{16 + 9} = \sqrt{25} = 5
\end{aligned}
$$

(x_1, y_1) is $(1, 5)$
(x_2, y_2) is $(5, 8)$

$\therefore$ length of line is 5 units.

Worked Example 2.2

If the distance between the points $(3, 4)$ and $(7, k)$ is $\sqrt{65}$ units, find the value of k.

Solution

Using the distance formula
$$d = \sqrt{65}$$
$d = \sqrt{(x_2-x_1)^2 + (y_2-y_1)^2}$ where $(x_1, y_1) = (3, 4)$
$(x_2, y_2) = (7, k)$

$\therefore \sqrt{(7-3)^2 + (k-4)^2} = \sqrt{65}$

Square both sides to eliminate $\sqrt{}$ sign

$(7-3)^2 + (k-4)^2 = 65$

$4^2 + (k-4)^2 = 65$

$16 + (k-4)^2 = 65$

$(k-4)^2 = 49$

Take $\sqrt{}$ of both sides | Positive $\sqrt{}$ only since distance involved. |

$k - 4 = 7$

$k = 11$

The distance formula can be extended to 3-dimensions such that the distance d between (x_1, y_1, z_1) and (x_2, y_2, z_2) is

$$d = \sqrt{(x_2-x_1)^2 + (y_2-y_1)^2 + (z_2-z_1)^2}$$

Mid-Point Formula

The point M which lies **exactly** halfway between (x_1, y_1) and (x_2, y_2) is given by

$$M\left(\frac{x_1 + x_2}{2}, \frac{y_1 + y_2}{2}\right)$$

This is called the mid-point formula.

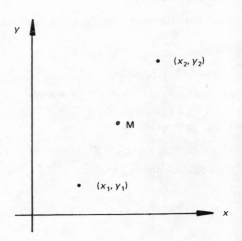

Worked Example 2.3

A rhombus has vertices $(-1, 4)$, $(4, 8)$, $(9, 4)$ and $(4, 0)$.

Find the co-ordinates of the point of intersection of the diagonals.

Solution

Diagonals **bisect** each other, i.e.
cut each other in half.

Co-ordinates are mid-point of
line joining

$(4, 0)$ and $(4, 8)$
or
$(-1, 4)$ and $(9, 4)$

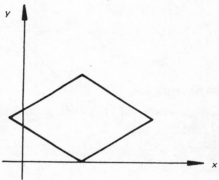

Point of intersection is $\left(\dfrac{4 + 4}{2}, \dfrac{0 + 8}{2} \right) = (4, 4)$

As with the distance formula, the mid-point formula can be extended to three dimensions as follows:

$$M\left(\frac{x_1 + x_2}{2}, \frac{y_1 + y_2}{2}, \frac{z_1 + z_2}{2} \right)$$

2.1.2   GRADIENT OF A LINE AND ITS PROPERTIES

The **gradient** of a line is simply a measure of the slope or steepness of the line.

Mathematically we wish to give the gradient a numerical value.

To do this we **must know** two points which lie on the line **or** the angle which the line makes with the x-axis.

Usually the letter m is used to denote the gradient of a line.

Given that any two points (x_1, y_1) and (x_2, y_2) the gradient of the line denoted by m is

$$m = \frac{y_2 - y_1}{x_2 - x_1}, \ x_1 \neq x_2$$

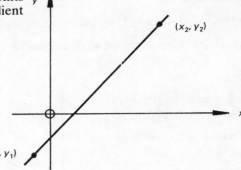

Worked Example 2.4

Calculate the gradient of the lines through the following points:

(a) (3, 7) and (5, 13)

(b) (6, 2) and (3, 8)

(c) (−3, 4) and (3, 4)

(d) (−2, −3) and (−2, 9)

Solution

(a) Using

$$m = \frac{y_2 - y_1}{x_2 - x_1} \text{ with } \begin{array}{l}(x_1, y_1) = (3, 7) \\ (x_2, y_2) = (5, 13)\end{array}$$

$$= \frac{13 - 7}{5 - 3} = \frac{6}{2} = 3$$

(b) Using

$$m = \frac{y_2 - y_1}{x_2 - x_1} \text{ with } \begin{array}{l}(x_1, y_1) = (6, 2) \\ (x_2, y_2) = (3, 8)\end{array}$$

$$= \frac{8 - 2}{3 - 6} = \frac{6}{-3} = -2$$

(c) Using

$$m = \frac{y_2 - y_1}{x_2 - x_1} \text{ with } \begin{array}{l}(x_1, y_1) = (-3, 4) \\ (x_2, y_2) = (3, 4)\end{array}$$

$$= \frac{4 - 4}{3 - (-3)} = \frac{0}{6} = 0$$

(d) Using

$$m = \frac{y_2 - y_1}{x_2 - x_1} \text{ with } \begin{array}{l}(x_1, y_1) = (-2, -3) \\ (x_2, y_2) = (-2, 9)\end{array}$$

$$= \frac{9 - (-3)}{-2 - (-2)} = \frac{12}{0} \text{ cannot divide by zero}$$

So m is undefined

From the previous examples it is obvious that there are 4 types of gradients which are described below.

A line with a **positive gradient** (i.e. $m > 0$) slopes up from left to right, i.e.

A line with a **negative gradient** (i.e. $m < 0$) slopes down from left to right, i.e.

A line with a **zero gradient** (i.e. $m = 0$) is horizontal, i.e.

A line with an **undefined gradient** (i.e. m undefined) is vertical, i.e.

If two lines with gradients m_1 and m_2 are parallel then $m_1 = m_2$

$m_1 = m_2 \Leftrightarrow$ lines are **parallel**

If two lines with gradients m_1 and m_2 are perpendicular then $m_1 m_2 = -1$

$m_1 m_2 = -1 \Leftrightarrow$ lines are **perpendicular**

Given that a line makes an angle of θ with the 'positive direction from the x-axis', the gradient of the line, m is given by

$$m = \tan \theta$$

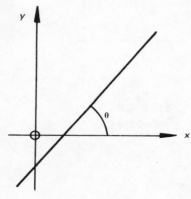

Note

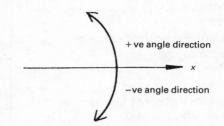

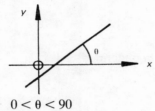

$0 < \theta < 90$
tan θ is +ve
∴ gradient positive

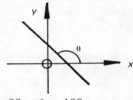

$90 < \theta < 180$
tan θ is −ve
∴ gradient −ve

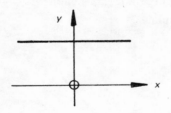

θ = 0
tan θ = 0
∴ gradient 0

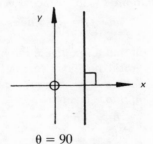

θ = 90
tan θ is undefined
∴ gradient undefined

Worked Example 2.5

What is the gradient of a line perpendicular to the line through the points P(4, 7) and Q(5, 11)?

Solution

$$m_{PQ} = \frac{11-7}{5-4} = \frac{4}{1} = 4$$

Gradient of perpendicular is m_2.

$$4m_2 = -1$$

$$\boxed{m_1 m_2 = -1 \text{ for perpendicular lines.}}$$

$$m_2 = -\frac{1}{4}$$

Worked Example 2.6

The line through the points $(-1, 3)$ and $(k, 4)$ is perpendicular to the line with gradient -3.

What is the value of k?

Solution

If $m_1 = -3$ then $m_2 = \frac{1}{3}$

$$\frac{4-3}{k-(-1)} = \frac{1}{3}$$

$$\frac{1}{k+1} = \frac{1}{3}$$

$$k+1 = 3$$

$$k = 2$$

Worked Example 2.7

Prove that the three points $A(1, -1)$, $B(3, 5)$ and $C(7, 17)$ are collinear.

Solution

> Collinear means lying on the **same** straight line.

If A, B and C are collinear then

$$m_{AB} = m_{BC} \qquad \boxed{\textbf{or} \quad m_{AB} = m_{AC}}$$

$$m_{AB} = \frac{5 - (-1)}{3 - 1} = \frac{6}{2} = 3$$

$$m_{BC} = \frac{17 - 5}{7 - 3} = \frac{12}{4} = 3$$

$\therefore$ Since $m_{AB} = m_{BC}$ and have a common point B, then A, B and C are collinear.

2.1.3   EQUATIONS OF A STRAIGHT LINE

From Standard Grade Mathematics you should already know that

$$y = mx + c$$

is the equation of a straight line where m is the gradient of a line **and**

$(0, c)$ is the y-intercept, i.e. the point where the line cuts the y-axis.

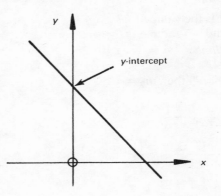

Worked Example 2.8

Write down the gradient and y-intercept for each straight line whose equation is given below.

(a) $y = 5x + 1$

(b) $y = 3 - x$

(c) $2y = 6x - 5$

(d) $4x + 3y = 8$

Solution

(a) $y = 5x + 1$ Here $m = 5$ and y-intercept is $(0, 1)$.

(b) $y = 3 - x$

   $= -x + 3$ Here $m = -1$ and y-intercept is $(0, 3)$

(c) $2y = 6x - 5$

   Need to divide both sides by 2

   $y = 3x - \dfrac{5}{2}$

> In order to find the gradient and y-intercept — equation must be written in the form $y = mx + c$

and so gradient is 3 and y- intercept is $\left(0, -\dfrac{5}{2}\right)$

(d) $4x + 3y = 8$

   Rearranging the equation

   $3y = -4x + 8$

   $y = -\dfrac{4}{3}x + \dfrac{8}{3}$

> Again equation must be in the form $y = mx + c$

and so gradient is $-\dfrac{4}{3}$

and y-intercept is $\left(0, \dfrac{8}{3}\right)$

Given the gradient of a straight line, m, and **any** point which lies on the line (x_1, y_1) — its equation is given by

   $y - y_1 = m(x - x_1)$

(Note this also applies to the above where (x_1, y_1) is $(0, c)$

   $y - c = m(x - 0)$

   $y - c = mx$

   $y = mx + c$

This is a very important equation which is extensively used in mathematics.

Worked Example 2.9

Determine the equation of the straight line with gradient 2 and passing through $(-1, 3)$.

Solution

Using $y - y_1 = m(x - x_1)$ with $m = 2$, $(x_1, y_1) = (-1, 3)$

$\Rightarrow y - 3 = 2(x - (-1))$

$\Rightarrow y - 3 = 2(x + 1)$

$\Rightarrow y - 3 = 2x + 2$

$\Rightarrow \quad y = 2x + 5$

Worked Example 2.10

Determine the equation of the straight line through the points $(4, 9)$ and $(6, -1)$.

Solution

> Here we must first evaluate the gradient m of the line before we can use $y - y_1 = m(x - x_1)$.

$m = \dfrac{-1 - 9}{6 - 4} = \dfrac{-10}{2} = -5$

The equation of the line using $\boxed{\text{Any of the two points may be used.}}$

$y - y_1 = m(x - x_1)$ with $m = -5$, $(x_1, y_1) = (4, 9)$

is $y - 9 = -5(x - 4)$

$\quad y - 9 = -5x + 20$

$5x + y - 29 = 0$ $\boxed{\textbf{or } 5x + y = 29 \textbf{ or } y = 29 - 5x}$

Worked Example 2.11

Find the equation of the line through the point $(-1, 3)$ which is parallel to the line with gradient 2.

Solution

$$\boxed{\text{Parallel lines have the same gradient}}$$

So gradient of required line is also 2.

$\therefore$ Equation of the line is

$$y - y_1 = m(x - x_1) \text{ with } m = 2 \text{ and } (x_1, y_1) = (-1, -3)$$
$$y - (-3) = 2(x - (-1))$$
$$y + 3 = 2(x + 1)$$
$$y + 3 = 2x + 2$$
$$2x - y - 1 = 0 \qquad \boxed{\textbf{or } y = 2x - 1 \textbf{ or } y - 2x + 1 = 0}$$

Worked Example 2.12

Find the equation of the line perpendicular to the line with gradient -4 and passing through $(2, -2)$.

Solution

$$\boxed{m_1 m_2 = -1 \text{ for perpendicular lines}}$$

Let gradient of required line be m.

$$-4m = -1$$
$$m = \frac{-1}{-4} = \frac{1}{4}$$

$\therefore$ Equation of line is

$$y - y_1 = m(x - x_1) \text{ with } m = \frac{1}{4} \text{ and } (x_1, y_1) = (2, -2)$$

$$\Rightarrow y - (-2) = \frac{1}{4}(x - 2)$$

$$\Rightarrow \quad y + 2 = \frac{1}{4}(x - 2) \qquad \boxed{\begin{array}{l}\text{Multiply through by 4}\\\text{to eliminate fraction}\end{array}}$$

$$\Rightarrow \quad 4y + 8 = x - 2$$
$$\Rightarrow x - 4y - 10 = 0 \qquad \boxed{\textbf{or } x - 4y = 10 \textbf{ or } 4y - x + 10 = 0}$$

Any straight line can be written in the form

$$Ax + By + C = 0 \text{——} *$$

This is called the **general equation of a straight line**.

Rearranging * into the form $y = mx + c$

$$Ax + By + C = 0$$
$$By = -Ax - C$$
$$y = -\frac{A}{B}x - \frac{C}{B}$$

Here $m = -\frac{A}{B}$

Worked Example 2.13

Determine the equation of the straight line passing through $(-4, -1)$ which is perpendicular to the line with equation $3x + 4y - 2 = 0$

Solution

Given the equation of a line $3x + 4y - 2 = 0$ we can easily find its gradient.

Using above information $m_1 = -\frac{3}{4}$

Line perpendicular to this line has gradient m_2.

So $-\frac{3}{4}m_2 = -1$

$$m_2 = -\frac{1}{-\frac{3}{4}} = \frac{4}{3}$$

$\therefore$ Equation of required line is

$$y - y_1 = m(x - x_1) \text{ with } m = \frac{4}{3} \text{ and } (x_1, y_1) = (-4, -1)$$

$\Rightarrow \qquad y - (-1) = \frac{4}{3}(x + 4)$ Multiply through by 3 to eliminate fraction

$\Rightarrow \qquad 3(y + 1) = 4(x + 4)$

$\Rightarrow \qquad 3y + 3 = 4x + 16$

$\Rightarrow 4x - 3y + 13 = 0$ $\boxed{\text{or } 3y - 4x - 13 = 0 \text{ or } 3y - 4x = 13}$

2.1.4   APPLICATIONS

The following facts concerning triangles must be known.

An **altitude** of a triangle is a
straight line drawn from a vertex
and is perpendicular to the
opposite side.

Every triangle has 3 altitudes.

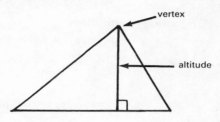

A **median** of a triangle is a
straight line drawn from a vertex
to the mid-point of the opposite
side.

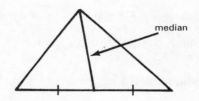

Worked Example 2.14

Triangle KLM has vertices with co-ordinates K(–2, 1), L(2, 3) and M(4, –3).
Find the equation of

(a) altitude drawn from K
       and
(b) median drawn from M.

Solution

(a) Remember to find equation we
       need to know gradient and a
       point which lies on the line.
       Here K lies on the line.
       Find gradient of LM — altitude
       is perpendicular to it.

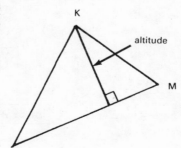

73

$$\therefore m_{LM} = \frac{-3-3}{4-2} = \frac{-6}{2} = -3$$

$$\boxed{\begin{array}{l} m_1 m_2 = -1 \\ -3m_2 = -1 \\ m_2 = \dfrac{1}{3} \end{array}}$$

$$\therefore \text{ gradient of altitude} = \frac{1}{3}$$

$\therefore$ Equation of altitude is

$$y - y_1 = m(x - x_1) \text{ with } (x_1, y_1) = (-2, 1)$$
$$m = \frac{1}{3}$$

$$y - 1 = \frac{1}{3}(x - (-2))$$

$$\Rightarrow \quad y - 1 = \frac{1}{3}(x + 2) \quad \boxed{\text{Multiply through by 3}}$$

$$\Rightarrow \quad 3(y - 1) = x + 2$$

$$\Rightarrow \quad 3y - 3 = x + 2$$

$$\Rightarrow x - 3y + 5 = 0 \quad \boxed{\textbf{or } 3y - x - 5 = 0 \textbf{ or } 3y = x + 5}$$

(b) Median passes through mid-point of KL.

$\therefore$ Mid-point is $\left(\dfrac{-2 + 2}{2}, \dfrac{1 + 3}{2}\right)$

$$= (0, 2)$$

$\therefore$ We want the equation of the line passing through the points $(4, -3)$ and $(0, 2)$.

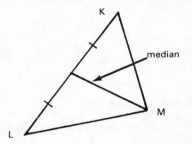

Firstly calculate the gradient

$$m = \frac{2 - (-3)}{0 - 4} = -\frac{5}{4}$$

The equation of the altitude is

$$\boxed{\begin{array}{l}\text{Using any of the two points} \\ \text{— we will use } (0, 2)\end{array}}$$

$$y - y_1 = m(x - x_1) \text{ with } m = -\frac{5}{4}$$
$$(x_1, y_1) = (0, 2)$$

$$y - 2 = -\frac{5}{4}(x - 0)$$

$$\Rightarrow \quad y - 2 = -\frac{5}{4}x \quad \boxed{\text{Multiply through by 4}}$$

$$\Rightarrow \quad 4(y - 2) = -5x$$

$$\Rightarrow \quad 4y - 2 = -5x$$

$$\Rightarrow 5x + 4y - 2 = 0 \quad \boxed{\textbf{or } 5x + 4y = 2}$$

Worked Example 2.15

A kite has vertices P(3, 5), Q(7, 2), R(3, −5) and S(−1, 2).
Find the equations of its diagonals.

Solution

Diagonals are lines joining points PR and QS.

| Think carefully about this one! | Diagonals are perpendicular!

Diagonal PR is vertical and has equation $x = 3$.
Diagonal QS is horizontal and has equation $y = 2$.

2.2 CO-ORDINATE GEOMETRY OF CIRCLES

2.2.1 BASIC FACTS

You should already be familiar with the basic terminology and properties
associated with circles.

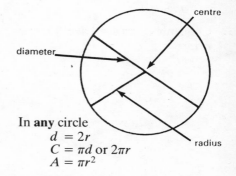

Perimeter of a circle is called the
circumference. It is usually denoted by
the letter C.

Diameter is the line between any two
points on the circumference through
the centre.

It is usually denoted by the letter d.

Radius is the line from centre of the
circle to the circumference.

It is usually denoted by the letter r.

In **any** circle
$$d = 2r$$
$$C = \pi d \text{ or } 2\pi r$$
$$A = \pi r^2$$

A **chord** is any line joining two points on the circumference. Diameter is a
chord.

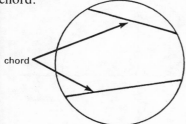

Any radius perpendicular to a
chord **bisects** it, i.e. cuts it into
2 equal parts.

75

A tangent to a circle is a straight line which meets the circumference at **one point** only.

The radius drawn to the point of contact of the tangent is perpendicular to it.

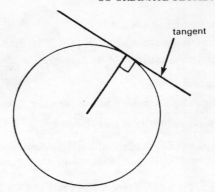

Concentric circles have the **same** centre.

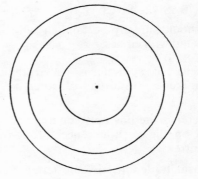

2.2.2 EQUATIONS OF A CIRCLE

From your previous studies in mathematics you know that

$$x^2 + y^2 = r^2$$

is the equation of any circle centre O and radius r.

If any point (x, y) lies

inside the circle then $x^2 + y^2 < r^2$

outside the circle then $x^2 + y^2 > r^2$

on the circumference then $x^2 + y^2 = r^2$

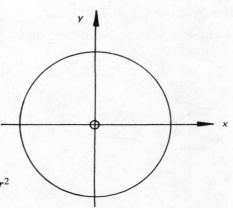

Worked Example 2.16

Write down the radius of each of the following circles

(a) $x^2 + y^2 = 16$ here $r^2 = 16 \Rightarrow r = \sqrt{16} = 4$

(b) $x^2 + y^2 = 50$ here $r^2 = 50 \Rightarrow r = \sqrt{50} = \sqrt{25 \times 2} = 5\sqrt{2}$

(c) $x^2 + y^2 = 23$ here $r^2 = 23 \Rightarrow r = \sqrt{23}$

Worked Example 2.17

Find the equation of the tangent to the circle $x^2 + y^2 = 34$ at the point $(3, 5)$.

Solution

> Tangent is a **straight line** — we require equation of a straight line and so need to calculate m. We **know** a point on the line, i.e. $(3, 5)$.

Gradient of radius, $m_{\text{radius}} = \dfrac{5-0}{3-0}$

$$= \frac{5}{3}$$

Since radius is perpendicular to tangent $\Rightarrow$ gradient of tangent is $-\dfrac{3}{5}$

$$\boxed{m_1 m_2 = -1}$$

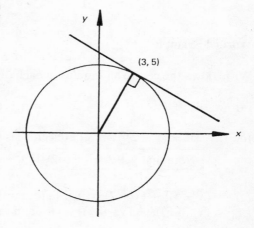

Equation of tangent is

$$y - y_1 = m(x - x_1) \text{ with } m = -\frac{3}{5}$$
$$\text{and } (x_1, y_1) = (3, 5)$$

$$y - 5 = -\frac{3}{5}(x - 3) \qquad \boxed{\text{Multiply through by 5}}$$

$\Rightarrow \qquad 5(y - 5) = -3(x - 3)$

$\Rightarrow \qquad 5y - 25 = -3x + 9$

$\Rightarrow 3x + 5y - 34 = 0 \qquad \boxed{\textbf{or } 3x + 5y = 34}$

The equation of any circle centre (a, b) and radius r is

$$(x-a)^2 + (y-b)^2 = r^2$$

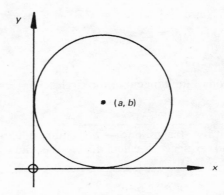

Worked Example 2.18

Write down the centre and radius of each of the following circles

(a) $(x-4)^2 + (y-1)^2 = 9$ here centre is $(4, 1)$ and radius $\sqrt{9} = 3$

(b) $(x-3)^2 + (y+2)^2 = 1$ here centre is $(3, -2)$ and radius $\sqrt{1} = 1$

> Note that $y + 2 = y - (-2)$

(c) $(x+5)^2 + (y+7)^2 = 8$ here centre is $(-5, -7)$
$\Rightarrow (x-(-5))^2 + (y-(-7))^2 = 8$ and radius $\sqrt{8} = 2\sqrt{2}$

(d) $x^2 + (y-6)^2 = 36$ here centre is $(0, 6)$
$\Rightarrow (x-0)^2 + (y-6)^2 = 36$ and radius is $\sqrt{36} = 6$

(e) $(x+4)^2 + y^2 = 23$ here centre is $(-4, 0)$
$\Rightarrow (x-(-4))^2 + (y-0)^2 = 23$ and radius is $\sqrt{23}$

Worked Example 2.19

Find the equation of the circle when a diameter has end points (3, 5) and (9, 7).

Solution

> To determine the equation of a circle we need to know the **centre** and the **radius**.
>
> In this case we can find both of these and so can establish the equation of the circle.

Centre is the mid-point of diameter — **use** mid-point formula

$$\therefore \text{ centre is } \left(\frac{3+9}{2}, \frac{5+7}{2}\right)$$
$$= (6, 6)$$

Radius is the distance between centre and **any** point on circumference — use distance formula

$$\therefore \text{radius } r = \sqrt{(6-3)^2 + (6-5)^2}$$
$$= \sqrt{3^2 + 1^2} = \sqrt{9+1} = \sqrt{10}$$

$\therefore$ Equation of circle is

$$(x-a)^2 + (y-b)^2 = r^2 \quad \text{with } (a, b) = (6, 6) \text{ and } r = \sqrt{10}$$
$$\Rightarrow (x-6)^2 + (y-6)^2 = 10$$

The general equation of **any** circle is of the form

$$x^2 + y^2 + 2gx + 2fy + c = 0 \qquad g^2 + f^2 - c \geqslant 0$$

where $(-g, -f)$ is the centre
and $\sqrt{g^2 + f^2 - c}$ is the radius.

Worked Example 2.20

Write down the centre and radius of the following circles

(a) $x^2 + y^2 + 6x + 8y + 5 = 0$

$$\left.\begin{array}{l}\text{Here } 2g = 6 \Rightarrow g = 3 \\ \qquad 2f = 8 \Rightarrow f = 4\end{array}\right\} \text{ centre is } (-3, -4)$$

and radius $= \sqrt{(-3)^2 + (-4)^2 - 5} = \sqrt{9 + 16 - 5} = \sqrt{20} = 2\sqrt{5}$

(b) $x^2 + y^2 - 10x + 5y - 3 = 0$ $\boxed{\text{Careful with sign!}}$

Here $2g = -10 \Rightarrow g = -5$
$\left. \right\}$ centre is $\left(5, -\dfrac{5}{2}\right)$
$2f = 5 \Rightarrow f = \dfrac{5}{2}$

and radius $= \sqrt{5^2 + \left(-\dfrac{5}{2}\right)^2 - (-3)}$

$= \sqrt{25 + \dfrac{25}{4} + 3} = \sqrt{\dfrac{100 + 25 + 12}{4}}$

$= \sqrt{\dfrac{137}{2}}$

(c) $2x^2 + 2y^2 - 8x - 14y + 9 = 0$

$\boxed{\text{The coefficients of } x^2 \text{ and } y^2 \textbf{ must be } 1 \text{ in order to obtain the centre and radius!}}$

Divide the above equation through by 2

$x^2 + y^2 - 4x - 7y + \dfrac{9}{2} = 0$

Here $2g = -4 \Rightarrow g = -2$
$\left. \right\}$ centre is $\left(2, \dfrac{7}{2}\right)$
$2f = -7 \Rightarrow f = -\dfrac{7}{2}$

and radius $= \sqrt{2^2 + \left(\dfrac{7}{2}\right)^2 - \dfrac{9}{2}}$

$= \sqrt{4 + \dfrac{49}{4} - \dfrac{9}{2}} = \sqrt{\dfrac{26 + 49 - 18}{4}}$

$= \sqrt{\dfrac{47}{4}} = \dfrac{\sqrt{47}}{2}$

(d) $3x^2 + 6y^2 + 7x - 11y - 5 = 0$

We **cannot** make the coefficients of x^2 and y^2 both 1 — so this **is not** the equation of a circle.

(e) $x^2 + y^2 + 10x - 2 = 0$

Here we have $x^2 + y^2 + 10x + 0y - 2 = 0$

and so $2g = 10 \Rightarrow g = 5$
$\left. \right\}$ centre is $(-5, 0)$
$2f = 0 \Rightarrow f = 0$

and radius $= \sqrt{(-5)^2 - (-2)}$
$= \sqrt{25 + 2} = \sqrt{27}$

Worked Example 2.21

Find the equation of the circle concentric to the circle with equation $x^2 + y^2 + 12x - 8y + 3 = 0$ but has radius half that of the given circle.

Solution

Remember concentric circles have the same centre

Given $x^2 + y^2 + 12x - 8y + 3 = 0$

Here centre is $(-6, 4)$

and radius $= \sqrt{(-6)^2 + 4^2 - 3}$

$= \sqrt{36 + 16 - 3}$

$= \sqrt{49}$

$= 7$

$\therefore$ Centre and radius of required circle are $(-6, 4)$ and $\dfrac{7}{2}$ respectively.

$\therefore$ Equation of required circle is

$$(x - a)^2 + (y - b)^2 = r^2 \quad \text{with } (a, b) = (-6, 4) \text{ and } r = \frac{7}{2}$$

$$(x - (-6))^2 + (y - 4)^2 = \left(\frac{7}{2}\right)^2$$

$$\Rightarrow \quad (x + 6)^2 + (y - 4)^2 = \frac{49}{4} \qquad \boxed{\text{Multiply by 4}}$$

$$\Rightarrow 4(x + 6)^2 + 4(y - 4)^2 = 49$$

To get in format of * expand and simplify.

$$4(x^2 + 12x + 36) + 4(y^2 - 8y + 16) = 49$$

$$4x^2 + 4y^2 + 48x - 32y + 144 + 64 - 49 = 0$$

i.e. $\qquad\qquad 4x^2 + 4y^2 + 48x - 32y + 159 = 0$

2.2.3   APPLICATIONS

Worked Example 2.22

Show that the line with equation $x + y - 12 = 0$ is a tangent to the circle $x^2 + y^2 + 8x - 12y + 2 = 0$ and find the co-ordinates of the point of contact.

Solution

Solving the system if equations
$$x + y - 12 = 0 \text{——①}$$
$$x^2 + y^2 + 8x - 12y + 2 = 0 \text{——②}$$

Rewriting equation ① as $y = 12 - x$ and substituting this expression for y into equation ②

$x^2 + (12 - x)^2 + 8x - 12(12 - x) + 2 = 0$

$\Rightarrow x^2 + 144 - 24x + x^2 + 8x - 144 + 12x + 2 = 0$

$\Rightarrow 2x^2 - 4x + 2 = 0$

$\Rightarrow 2(x^2 - 2x + 1) = 0$

$\Rightarrow x^2 - 2x + 1 = 0$

$\Rightarrow (x - 1)^2 = 0$

$\Rightarrow x = 1$

> Since '$b^2 - 4ac$' $= 0$ there is only **one** point of contact so line is a tangent to circle.

When $x = 1$, $y = 12 - 1 = 11$

$\therefore$ Point of contact is $(1, 11)$

This process is used when you want to find the point(s) of contact of a line and any curve.

Worked Example 2.23

Find the point(s) of contact where the line $2x - y + 3 = 0$ meets the curve $x^2 + 3y^2 = 36$

Solution

Solving the system of equations
$$2x - y + 3 = 0 \text{——①}$$
$$x^2 + 3y^2 = 36 \text{——②}$$

Rewriting equation ① as $y = 2x + 3$ and substituting this expression for y into equation ②.

$$x^2 + 3(2x + 3)^2 = 36$$
$$\Rightarrow \quad x^2 + 3(4x^2 + 12x + 9) = 36$$
$$\Rightarrow \quad x^2 + 12x^2 + 36x + 27 - 36 = 0$$
$$\Rightarrow \quad 13x^2 + 36x - 9 = 0$$
$$\Rightarrow (13x - 3)(x + 3) = 0$$
$$\Rightarrow \quad 13x - 3 = 0 \text{ or } x + 3 = 0$$
$$\Rightarrow \quad x = \frac{3}{13} \text{ or } -3$$

When $x = \frac{3}{13}$, $y = 2\left(\frac{3}{13}\right) + 3 = \frac{6}{13} + \frac{39}{13} = \frac{45}{13}$

$$x = -3, y = 2(-3) + 3 = -3$$

$\therefore$ points of contact are $\left(\frac{3}{13}, \frac{45}{13}\right)$ and $(-3, -3)$.

Worked Example 2.24

A is the point (9, 2), B is (−1, −6) and C is (−1, 2).

(a) Find the equations of the chords AB and BC.

(b) Hence find the centre of the circle.

(c) Determine the radius of the circle.

(d) Find the equation of the circle which passes through A, B and C.

Solution

(a)

Since chords are straight lines and we know two points on each of the lines → equations can be easily found.

Chord AB

$$m_{AB} = \frac{-6 - 2}{1 - (9)} = \frac{-8}{-8} = 1$$

Using $y - y_1 = m(x - x_1)$ | Use either (9, 2) or (−1, −6) |

Equation of AB is

$$y - 2 = 1(x - (9))$$
$$\Rightarrow y - 2 = x - 9$$
$$\Rightarrow x - y - 7 = 0$$

Chord BC

$$m_{BC} = \frac{2-(-6)}{-1-(-1)} = \frac{8}{0} \text{ is undefined.}$$

∴ Equation of BC is $x = -1$ | Undefined gradient ⇔ vertical line |

(b) | The perpendicular bisector of a chord in any circle passes through the **centre**.

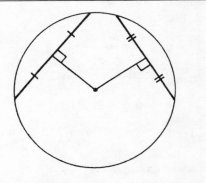

By finding equation of perpendicular bisector of AB and BC, the centre of the circle can be determined by solving the simultaneous equations.

Perpendicular bisector of AB

$m_{AB} = 1$ so gradient required $m_1 = -1$

Mid-point of AB is $\left(\frac{9-1}{2}, \frac{2-6}{2}\right) = (4, -2)$

∴ Equation of perpendicular bisector is

$$y - (-2) = -1(x - (4))$$
$$\Rightarrow y + 2 = -x + 4$$
$$\Rightarrow x + y - 2 = 0$$

Perpendicular bisector of BC

m_{BC} is undefined ⇔ line is vertical.

Perpendicular line is horizontal ⇔ $m = 0$

Mid-point of BC is $\left(\frac{-1 + (-1)}{2}, \frac{-6 + 2}{2}\right) = (-1, -2)$

∴ Equation of perpendicular bisector is $y = -2$

Solving $x + y + 7 = 0$ —— ①

$y = -2$ —— ②

$\Rightarrow x - 2 + 7 = 0 \Rightarrow x = -5$

Centre of circle = solution of simultaneous equations

$= (-5, 7)$

(c)

> Radius can be calculated by finding the length of the line from the centre $(-2, -2)$ to **any one** of the points A, B or C.

$\text{radius} = \sqrt{(-5 - (-1))^2 + (7 - 2)^2}$ $\boxed{\text{Using } C(-1, 2)}$

$= \sqrt{(-4)^2 + (5)^2}$

$= \sqrt{16 + 25}$

$= \sqrt{41}$ units

(d) Using $(x - a)^2 + (y - b)^2 = r^2$ where (a, b) is $(-5, -2)$ and $r = \sqrt{41}$ units.
The equation of the circle is

$(x - (-5))^2 + (y - (7))^2 = (\sqrt{41})^2$

$(x + 5)^2 + (y - 7)^2 = 41$ ——— *

or $x^2 + y^2 + 10x - 14y - 33 = 0$ (found by expanding *)

Worked Example 2.25

Show that the circle passing through the points $(-6, 0)$, $(0, 0)$ and $(0, 6)$ has equation $x^2 + y^2 + 6x - 6y = 0$

Solution

From equation centre of circle is $(-3, 3)$. This is the mid-point of line joining $(-6, 0)$ and $(0, 6)$.

$\therefore$ End-points of diameter of circle are $(-6, 0)$ and $(0, 6)$.

Centre of circle is known. Radius is length of line from $(-3, 3)$ to $(-6, 0)$ or $(0, 6)$.

$\therefore \text{radius} = \sqrt{(-3 - 0)^2 + (3 - 6)^2}$

$= \sqrt{(-3)^2 + (-3)^2}$

$= \sqrt{9 + 9} = \sqrt{18} = \sqrt{9 \times 2} = 3\sqrt{2}$ units

$\therefore$ Equation of circle is

$(x - (-3))^2 + (y - 3)^2 = (3\sqrt{2})^2$

$\Rightarrow (x + 3)^2 + (y - 3)^2 = 18$

$\Rightarrow x^2 + 6x + 9 + y^2 - 6y + 9 = 18$

$\Rightarrow x^2 + y^2 + 6x - 6y + 18 = 18$

$\Rightarrow x^2 + y^2 + 6x - 6y = 0$

    as required

2.3 VECTORS

2.3.1 BASIC PROPERTIES OF VECTORS

A **vector** is a directed line segment having both a magnitude (length) and direction.

There are a number of ways of representing vectors, the main ones being listed below.

Method I

This vector can be represented as $\overrightarrow{AB}$.

The arrow above the letters indicating the direction.

This vector can be represented by $\overrightarrow{BA}$

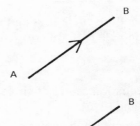

Note the vector $\overrightarrow{AB}$ above can also be represented by $\overleftarrow{BA}$. The arrow always indicates direction

Also $\overrightarrow{AB} = -\overrightarrow{BA}$ the minus sign changes direction of the vector.

Method II

A small letter written in bold type or underlined is also used to represent a vector.

Method III

Components can also be used to represent vectors.

Two dimensional vectors require two components $\begin{pmatrix} x \\ y \end{pmatrix}$.

Three dimensional vectors require three components $\begin{pmatrix} x \\ y \\ z \end{pmatrix}$.

It is usual for two of the above methods to be used together, e.g.

$$\underline{a} = \begin{pmatrix} 4 \\ 7 \end{pmatrix} \qquad \overrightarrow{MN} = \begin{pmatrix} -1 \\ 0 \\ 5 \end{pmatrix}$$

The length of a vector is known as the **magnitude** and given a vector

 (i) $\underline{a}$ the magnitude is written as $|\underline{a}|$.

(ii) $\overrightarrow{AB}$ the magnitude is written as $|\overrightarrow{AB}|$.

To calculate the magnitude of a vector we must know the components.

In 2-dimensions if $\underline{a} = \begin{pmatrix} x \\ y \end{pmatrix}$ then $|\underline{a}| = \sqrt{x^2 + y^2}$

In 3-dimensions if $\underline{a} = \begin{pmatrix} x \\ y \\ z \end{pmatrix}$ then $|\underline{a}| = \sqrt{x^2 + y^2 + z^2}$

Worked Example 2.26

Calculate the magnitude of each of the following vectors.

(a) $\underline{p} = \begin{pmatrix} 3 \\ 4 \end{pmatrix}$

(b) $\overrightarrow{KL} = \begin{pmatrix} -2 \\ 0 \end{pmatrix}$

(c) $\overrightarrow{EF} = \begin{pmatrix} -1 \\ 1 \\ -2 \end{pmatrix}$

(d) $\underline{m} = \begin{pmatrix} 0 \\ -5 \\ 6 \end{pmatrix}$

Solution

(a) If $\underline{p} = \begin{pmatrix} 3 \\ 4 \end{pmatrix}$ then $|\underline{p}| = \sqrt{3^2 + 4^2}$
$$= \sqrt{9 + 16} = \sqrt{25} = 5$$

(b) If $\overrightarrow{KL} = \begin{pmatrix} -2 \\ 0 \end{pmatrix}$ then $|\overrightarrow{KL}| = \sqrt{(-2)^2 + 0^2}$
$$= \sqrt{4 + 0} = \sqrt{4} = 2$$

(c) If $\overrightarrow{EF} = \begin{pmatrix} -1 \\ 1 \\ -2 \end{pmatrix}$ then $|\overrightarrow{EF}| = \sqrt{(-1)^2 + 1^2 + (-2)^2}$
$$= \sqrt{1 + 1 + 4} = \sqrt{6}$$

(d) If $\underline{m} = \begin{pmatrix} 0 \\ -5 \\ 6 \end{pmatrix}$ then $|\underline{m}| = \sqrt{0^2 + (-5)^2 + 6^2}$
$$= \sqrt{0 + 25 + 36} = \sqrt{61}$$

A **unit vector** is any vector which has magnitude 1.

Worked Example 2.27

If $\underline{t} = \begin{pmatrix} k \\ 1 \\ \frac{1}{2} \end{pmatrix}$ is a unit vector find the value(s) of k.

Solution

If $\underline{t}$ is a unit vector the $|\underline{t}| = 1$.

So $\sqrt{k^2 + \frac{1}{2}^2} = 1$

$\Rightarrow \sqrt{k^2 + \frac{1}{4}} = 1$ | Squaring both sides to eliminate $\sqrt{}$

$\Rightarrow \quad k^2 + \frac{1}{4} = 1$

$\Rightarrow \quad k^2 = \frac{3}{4}$ | Take square root of both sides

$\Rightarrow \quad k = \pm \sqrt{\frac{3}{4}}$ | $\sqrt{\frac{3}{4}} = \frac{\sqrt{3}}{\sqrt{4}} = \frac{\sqrt{3}}{2}$

$\quad\quad\quad = \pm \frac{\sqrt{3}}{2}$

Vectors can also be written in the form
$$a\underline{i} + b\underline{j} + c\underline{k}$$
where $\underline{i}, \underline{j}$ and $\underline{k}$ are unit vectors, such that
$$a\underline{i} + b\underline{j} + c\underline{k} \equiv \begin{pmatrix} a \\ b \\ c \end{pmatrix}$$

2.3.2 VECTORS AND COMPONENTS

Vectors can be added as the following shows

$$\vec{PQ} + \vec{QR} = \vec{PR}$$

i.e. path taken from P to Q
followed by that from Q to R
would take you to the same
'point' as the path from P to R.

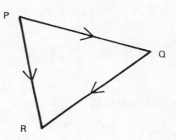

With components if $\vec{PQ} = \begin{pmatrix} a_1 \\ b_1 \end{pmatrix}$ and $\vec{QR} = \begin{pmatrix} a_2 \\ b_2 \end{pmatrix}$

then $\vec{PQ} + \vec{QR} = \begin{pmatrix} a_1 \\ b_1 \end{pmatrix} + \begin{pmatrix} a_2 \\ b_2 \end{pmatrix} = \begin{pmatrix} a_1 + a_2 \\ b_1 + b_2 \end{pmatrix}$

So $\vec{PR} = \begin{pmatrix} a_1 + a_2 \\ b_1 + b_2 \end{pmatrix}$

Worked Example 2.28

If $\vec{KL} = \begin{pmatrix} 5 \\ 0 \\ -2 \end{pmatrix}$ and $\vec{LM} = \begin{pmatrix} -1 \\ 4 \\ 3 \end{pmatrix}$

Evaluate *(a)* $\vec{KM}$ and *(b)* $\vec{MK}$

Solution

(a) $\vec{KM} = \vec{KL} + \vec{LM} = \begin{pmatrix} 5 \\ 0 \\ -2 \end{pmatrix} + \begin{pmatrix} -1 \\ 4 \\ 3 \end{pmatrix} = \begin{pmatrix} 5 + (-1) \\ 0 + 4 \\ -2 + 3 \end{pmatrix} = \begin{pmatrix} 4 \\ 4 \\ 1 \end{pmatrix}$

(b) $\vec{MK} = -\vec{KM} = - \begin{pmatrix} 4 \\ 4 \\ 1 \end{pmatrix} = \begin{pmatrix} -4 \\ -4 \\ -1 \end{pmatrix}$

From the last example we can 'multiply' a vector by a scalar.

Note: a scalar has magnitude only but **no** direction.

So if $p = \begin{pmatrix} a \\ b \\ c \end{pmatrix}$ and k is a scalar then

$$kp = k \begin{pmatrix} a \\ b \\ c \end{pmatrix} = \begin{pmatrix} ka \\ kb \\ kc \end{pmatrix}$$

Worked Example 2.29

If $p = \begin{pmatrix} -2 \\ 5 \end{pmatrix}$, $q = \begin{pmatrix} 3 \\ 11 \\ -4 \end{pmatrix}$ and $r = \begin{pmatrix} 0 \\ -6 \end{pmatrix}$

find   *(a)* $3p$ *(b)* $-q$ *(c)* $-6r$ *(d)* $\frac{1}{5}p$

Solution

(a) $3p = 3\begin{pmatrix} -2 \\ 5 \end{pmatrix} = \begin{pmatrix} -6 \\ 15 \end{pmatrix}$

(b) $-q = -\begin{pmatrix} 3 \\ 11 \\ -4 \end{pmatrix} = \begin{pmatrix} -3 \\ -11 \\ 4 \end{pmatrix}$

(c) $-6r = -6\begin{pmatrix} 0 \\ -6 \end{pmatrix} = \begin{pmatrix} 0 \\ 36 \end{pmatrix}$

(d) $\frac{1}{5}p = \frac{1}{5}\begin{pmatrix} -2 \\ 5 \end{pmatrix} = \begin{pmatrix} -\frac{2}{5} \\ 1 \end{pmatrix}$

Worked Example 2.30

If $a = 3i + 2j - k$ and $b = 5i + 4k$

Find   *(a)* $3a + b$ *(b)* $2a - 3b$

Solution

When $\underline{a} = 3\underline{i} + 2\underline{j} - \underline{k} \Leftrightarrow \underline{a} = \begin{pmatrix} 3 \\ 2 \\ -1 \end{pmatrix}$

and $\underline{b} = 5\underline{i} + 4\underline{k} = 5\underline{i} + 0\underline{j} + 4\underline{k} \Leftrightarrow \underline{b} = \begin{pmatrix} 5 \\ 0 \\ 4 \end{pmatrix}$

So

(a) $3\underline{a} + \underline{b} = 3 \begin{pmatrix} 3 \\ 2 \\ -1 \end{pmatrix} + \begin{pmatrix} 5 \\ 0 \\ 4 \end{pmatrix} = \begin{pmatrix} 9 + 5 \\ 6 + 0 \\ -3 + 4 \end{pmatrix} = \begin{pmatrix} 14 \\ 6 \\ 1 \end{pmatrix}$

$\therefore 3\underline{a} + \underline{b} = 14\underline{i} + 6\underline{j} + \underline{k}$

(b) $2\underline{a} - 3\underline{b} = 2 \begin{pmatrix} 3 \\ 2 \\ -1 \end{pmatrix} - 3 \begin{pmatrix} 5 \\ 0 \\ 4 \end{pmatrix} = \begin{pmatrix} 6 - 15 \\ 4 - 0 \\ -2 - 12 \end{pmatrix} = \begin{pmatrix} -9 \\ 4 \\ -14 \end{pmatrix}$

$\therefore 2\underline{a} - 3\underline{b} = -9\underline{i} + 4\underline{j} - 14\underline{k}$

This could also have been done without going into components, i.e.

$3\underline{a} + \underline{b} = 3(3\underline{i} + 2\underline{j} - \underline{k}) + (5\underline{i} + 4\underline{k})$

$\qquad\qquad = 9\underline{i} + 6\underline{j} - 3\underline{k} + 5\underline{i} + 4\underline{k}$

$\qquad\qquad = 9\underline{i} + 5\underline{i} + 6\underline{j} - 3\underline{k} + 4\underline{k}$

$\qquad\qquad = 14\underline{i} + 6\underline{j} + \underline{k}$

as above

Position vectors are a very important part of vector geometry.

Given the co-ordinates of any point P(a, b), the vector from the origin to the point P is called the **position vector** of P denoted by $\overrightarrow{OP}$ or $\underline{p}$ with components $\begin{pmatrix} a \\ b \end{pmatrix}$.

Any point can be represented by a position vector.

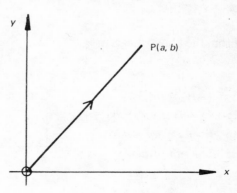

Furthermore any vector can be represented by position vectors as shown below.

$$\overrightarrow{PQ} = \overrightarrow{PO} + \overrightarrow{OQ} \qquad \overrightarrow{OP} = \underline{p}$$

$$= -\underline{p} + \underline{q} \qquad \text{so } \overrightarrow{PO} = -\underline{p}$$

$$= \underline{q} - \underline{p}$$

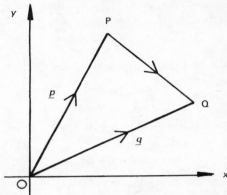

In general
$$\overrightarrow{AB} = \underline{b} - \underline{a}$$

The mid-point of vector $\overrightarrow{AB}$ is

$$\frac{1}{2}(\underline{a} + \underline{b})$$

in terms of position vectors

If some point B divides the line AC in the ratio $m : n$, position vectors can be used to find the point B given the co-ordinates of A and C and the ratio $m : n$.

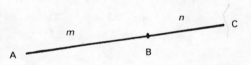

From the above diagram

$$\frac{AB}{BC} = \frac{m}{n}$$

So $n(\overrightarrow{AB}) = m(\overrightarrow{BC})$

$\Rightarrow n(\underline{b} - \underline{a}) = m(\underline{c} - \underline{b})$

$\Rightarrow n\underline{b} - n\underline{a} = m\underline{c} - m\underline{b}$

$\Rightarrow n\underline{b} + m\underline{b} = m\underline{c} + n\underline{a}$

$\Rightarrow \qquad \underline{b} = \dfrac{m\underline{c} + n\underline{a}}{m + n}$

It can easily be remembered as

A   C
$\times$
$m : n$

Worked Example 2.31

If the line joining the points A(0, 5) and C(−3, 2) is divided in the ratio 2:1 by the point B, find the co-ordinates of B.

Solution

$$\frac{AB}{BC} = \frac{2}{1}$$

So $\overrightarrow{AB} = 2(\overrightarrow{BC})$

$\Rightarrow \quad \underline{b} - \underline{a} = 2(\underline{c} - \underline{b})$

$\Rightarrow \quad \underline{b} - \underline{a} = 2\underline{c} - 2\underline{b}$

$\Rightarrow \underline{b} + 2\underline{b} = 2\underline{c} + \underline{a}$

$\Rightarrow \quad \quad 3\underline{b} = 2\underline{c} + \underline{a}$

$\Rightarrow \quad \quad \underline{b} = \frac{1}{3}(2\underline{c} + \underline{a}) \quad$ with $\underline{a} = \begin{pmatrix} 0 \\ 5 \end{pmatrix}, \underline{c} = \begin{pmatrix} -3 \\ 2 \end{pmatrix}$

$$= \frac{1}{3}\left[2\begin{pmatrix} -3 \\ 2 \end{pmatrix} + \begin{pmatrix} 0 \\ 5 \end{pmatrix} \right]$$

$$= \frac{1}{3}\left[\begin{pmatrix} -6 + 0 \\ 4 + 5 \end{pmatrix} \right]$$

$$= \frac{1}{3}\begin{pmatrix} -6 \\ 9 \end{pmatrix} = \begin{pmatrix} -2 \\ 3 \end{pmatrix}$$

$\therefore$ B is the point (−2, 3)

Worked Example 2.32

The points P(6, −2, 0) and R(1, 3, 5) are divided in the ratio 2:3 by the point Q.

What are the co-ordinates of Q?

Solution

$$\frac{PQ}{PR} = \frac{2}{3}$$

So $3\overrightarrow{PQ} = 2\overrightarrow{QR}$

$$\Rightarrow 3(\underline{q} - \underline{p}) = 2(\underline{r} - \underline{q})$$
$$\Rightarrow 3\underline{q} - 3\underline{p} = 2\underline{r} - 2\underline{q}$$
$$\Rightarrow 3\underline{q} + 2\underline{q} = 2\underline{r} + 3\underline{p}$$
$$\Rightarrow \qquad 5\underline{q} = 2\underline{r} + 3\underline{p}$$

$$\Rightarrow \qquad \underline{q} = \frac{1}{5}(2\underline{r} + 3\underline{p}) \qquad \text{with } \underline{p} = \begin{pmatrix} 6 \\ -2 \\ 0 \end{pmatrix}, \underline{r} = \begin{pmatrix} 1 \\ 3 \\ 5 \end{pmatrix}$$

$$= \frac{1}{5}\left[2\begin{pmatrix} 1 \\ 3 \\ 5 \end{pmatrix} + 3\begin{pmatrix} 6 \\ -2 \\ 0 \end{pmatrix} \right]$$

$$= \frac{1}{5}\begin{pmatrix} 2 + 18 \\ 6 - 6 \\ 10 + 0 \end{pmatrix} = \frac{1}{5}\begin{pmatrix} 20 \\ 0 \\ 10 \end{pmatrix} = \begin{pmatrix} 4 \\ 0 \\ 2 \end{pmatrix}$$

$\therefore$ Q is the point $(4, 0, 2)$

Vectors can also be used to prove that 3 points in 3 dimensions are collinear, i.e. lie on the same line.

> They can also be used to show that 3 points in 2 dimensions are collinear or you can use gradients as seen in section 2.1.

If P, Q and R are collinear then $\overrightarrow{PQ}$ is a multiple of $\overrightarrow{QR}$, i.e. $\overrightarrow{PQ} = k\overrightarrow{QR}$ and vice versa.

Worked Example 2.33

Prove that the points $P(3, -1, 2)$, $Q(4, 0, -3)$ and $R(6, 2, -13)$ are collinear.

Solution

Need to show that $\overrightarrow{PQ} = k\overrightarrow{QR}$.

$$\overrightarrow{PQ} = \underline{q} - \underline{p} = \begin{pmatrix} 4 \\ 0 \\ -3 \end{pmatrix} - \begin{pmatrix} 3 \\ -1 \\ 2 \end{pmatrix} = \begin{pmatrix} 1 \\ 5 \\ -5 \end{pmatrix} \qquad \boxed{\text{Using position vectors}}$$

$$\overrightarrow{QR} = \underline{r} - \underline{q} = \begin{pmatrix} 6 \\ 2 \\ -13 \end{pmatrix} - \begin{pmatrix} 4 \\ 0 \\ -3 \end{pmatrix} = \begin{pmatrix} 1 \\ 2 \\ -10 \end{pmatrix} = 2\begin{pmatrix} 1 \\ 1 \\ -5 \end{pmatrix}$$

$\therefore \overrightarrow{PQ} = 2\overrightarrow{QR}$

and so PQ and R are collinear.

Worked Example 2.34

Prove that the points A, B and C with co-ordinates $(2, -3, 4)$, $(-1, -2, 3)$ and $(-10, 1, 0)$ respectively are collinear. What ratio does B divide AC into?

Solution

$$\overrightarrow{AB} = \underline{b} - \underline{a} = \begin{pmatrix} -1 \\ -2 \\ 3 \end{pmatrix} - \begin{pmatrix} 2 \\ -3 \\ 4 \end{pmatrix} = \begin{pmatrix} -3 \\ 1 \\ -1 \end{pmatrix} \qquad \boxed{\text{Using position vectors}}$$

$$\overrightarrow{BC} = \underline{c} - \underline{b} = \begin{pmatrix} -10 \\ 1 \\ 0 \end{pmatrix} - \begin{pmatrix} -1 \\ -2 \\ 3 \end{pmatrix} = \begin{pmatrix} -9 \\ 3 \\ -3 \end{pmatrix} = 3 \begin{pmatrix} -3 \\ 1 \\ -1 \end{pmatrix}$$

$$\therefore \overrightarrow{AB} = 3\overrightarrow{BC}$$

and so A, B and C are collinear.

B divides AC in the ratio 1:3.

Since $\overrightarrow{AB} = 3\overrightarrow{BC}$

$\therefore$ ratio 1:3

2.3.3   SCALAR (DOT) PRODUCT

Given any two vectors $\underline{a}$ and $\underline{b}$ and the angle θ between them, the dot or scalar product is given by

$$\underline{a} \cdot \underline{b} = |\underline{a}||\underline{b}| \cos \theta$$

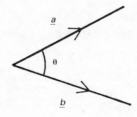

From the above diagram **note** the direction of the vectors $\underline{a}$ and $\underline{b}$.

There are **2 other cases**.

(i) In this case

$$\underline{a} \cdot \underline{b} = |\underline{a}| \, |\underline{b}| \cos \theta$$

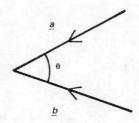

(ii)

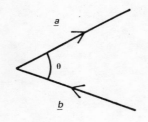   OR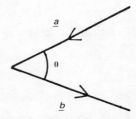

In these cases

$$\underline{a} \cdot \underline{b} = |\underline{a}| \, |\underline{b}| \cos (180 - \theta) \qquad \boxed{\cos (180 - \theta) = -\cos \theta}$$
$$= -|\underline{a}| \, |\underline{b}| \cos \theta$$

However given the components of $\underline{a}$ and $\underline{b}$ as $\begin{pmatrix} a_1 \\ a_2 \\ a_3 \end{pmatrix}$ and $\begin{pmatrix} b_1 \\ b_2 \\ b_3 \end{pmatrix}$ respectively then

$$\underline{a} \cdot \underline{b} = a_1 b_1 + a_2 b_2 + a_3 b_3$$

Since both result in the product $\underline{a} \cdot \underline{b}$ then

$$|\underline{a}| \, |\underline{b}| \cos \theta = a_1 b_1 + a_2 b_2 + a_3 b_3$$

So $\cos \theta = \dfrac{a_1 b_1 + a_2 b_2 + a_3 b_3}{|\underline{a}| \, |\underline{b}|}$

This can be used to find the angle θ between any two vectors.

Worked Example 2.35

If S and T are the points (2, 3, 4) and (−2, 0, 3) respectively, calculate the angle θ between vectors $\underline{s}$ and $\underline{t}$.

Solution

If $\underline{s} = \begin{pmatrix} 2 \\ 3 \\ 4 \end{pmatrix}$ then $|\underline{s}| = \sqrt{2^2 + 3^2 + 4^2}$

$$= \sqrt{4 + 9 + 16} = \sqrt{29}$$

and $\underline{t} = \begin{pmatrix} -2 \\ 0 \\ 3 \end{pmatrix}$ then $|\underline{t}| = \sqrt{(-2)^2 + 0^2 + 3^2}$

$$= \sqrt{4 + 0 + 9} = \sqrt{13}$$

$$\therefore \cos\theta = \frac{2 \times (-2) + 3 \times 0 + 4 \times 3}{\sqrt{29} \cdot \sqrt{13}}$$

$$= \frac{-4 + 0 + 12}{\sqrt{29} \cdot \sqrt{13}}$$

$$= \frac{8}{\sqrt{377}}$$

$$\therefore \theta = \cos^{-1}\left(\frac{8}{\sqrt{377}}\right) = 65 \cdot 7°$$

If the angle between 2 vectors = 90°, i.e. they are perpendicular, then $\theta = 90$.

$$\therefore \underline{a} \cdot \underline{b} = |\underline{a}||\underline{b}| \cos\theta \qquad \boxed{\cos 90° = 0}$$

$$= |\underline{a}||\underline{b}| \cos 90$$

$$= 0$$

Perpendicular vectors $\Leftrightarrow \underline{a} \cdot \underline{b} = 0$

Worked Example 2.36

Show that the vectors $\underline{p}$ and $\underline{q}$ with components $\begin{pmatrix} 4 \\ -1 \\ 1 \end{pmatrix}$ and $\begin{pmatrix} 1 \\ 2 \\ -2 \end{pmatrix}$ are perpendicular.

Solution

$$p \cdot q = (4 \times 1) + (-1 \times 2) + (1 \times (-2))$$
$$= 4 - 2 - 2$$
$$= 0$$

since $p \cdot q = 0$

$\Rightarrow p$ and q are perpendicular.

Worked Example 2.37

If the vectors $m = 3i - j + 2k$ and $n = ai - 5j - 4k$ are perpendicular, find the value of a.

Solution

Since m and n are perpendicular then $m \cdot n = 0$

$$m = \begin{pmatrix} 3 \\ -1 \\ 2 \end{pmatrix} \qquad n = \begin{pmatrix} a \\ -5 \\ -4 \end{pmatrix}$$

So $m \cdot n = 3a + 5 - 8 = 3a - 3$

$\therefore 3a - 3 = 0$

$$3a = 3$$
$$a = 1$$

Note that

$$a \cdot (a + b + c) = a \cdot a + a \cdot b + a \cdot c$$

where $a \cdot a = |a||a| \cos \theta \qquad \theta = 0°$

$$= |a||a| \cos 0 \qquad \cos 0 = 1$$
$$= |a||a|$$
$$= |a|^2$$

TRIGONOMETRY

3.1   REVISION

3.1.1   Right-angled △ Trigonometry

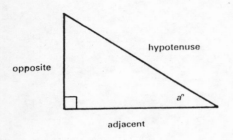

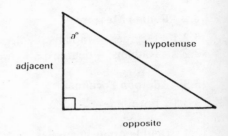

From the above △s we define the trig. ratios

| sin ≡ sine |

$$\sin a° = \frac{\text{opposite}}{\text{hypotenuse}}$$

| cos ≡ cosine |

$$\cos a° = \frac{\text{adjacent}}{\text{hypotenuse}}$$

| tan ≡ tangent |

$$\tan a° = \frac{\text{opposite}}{\text{adjacent}}$$

> **1**
> **Note that**
> $$\tan a° = \frac{\sin a°}{\cos a°}$$

The trig. ratios can be
abbreviated to SOHCAHTOA

'Proof of 1'

$$\frac{\sin a°}{\cos a°} = \frac{\dfrac{\text{opp}}{\text{hyp}}}{\dfrac{\text{adj}}{\text{hyp}}} = \frac{\text{opp}}{\text{hyp}} \times \frac{\text{hyp}}{\text{adj}} = \frac{\text{opp}}{\text{adj}} = \tan a°$$

We write $(\sin x°)^2 = \sin^2 x°$

and $(\cos x°)^2 = \cos^2 x°$ similarly $(\cos x°)^5 = \cos^5 x°$

> **2**
> **Note that**
> $$\sin^2 x + \cos^2 x = 1$$

'Proof of 2'
$$\sin^2 x + \cos^2 x = 1$$

L.H.S. $\sin^2 x + \cos^2 x$

$$= (\sin x)^2 + (\cos x)^2$$

$$= \left(\frac{\text{opp}}{\text{hyp}}\right)^2 + \left(\frac{\text{adj}}{\text{hyp}}\right)^2$$

$$= \frac{\text{opp}^2}{\text{hyp}^2} + \frac{\text{adj}^2}{\text{hyp}^2}$$

$$= \frac{\text{opp}^2 + \text{adj}^2}{\text{hyp}^2}$$

$$= \frac{\text{hyp}^2}{\text{hyp}^2}$$

$$= 1$$

$$\left(\tfrac{1}{2}\right)^2 = \tfrac{1}{2} \times \tfrac{1}{2} = \tfrac{1^2}{2^2}$$

$$\left(\tfrac{a}{b}\right)^2 = \tfrac{a^2}{b^2}$$

$$\tfrac{1}{2} + \tfrac{1}{3} \leftarrow \text{can't do simple addition}$$

$$\tfrac{1}{3} + \tfrac{2}{3} = \tfrac{1+2}{3}$$

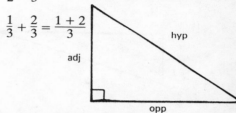

Using Pythagoras' Theorem
$$\text{hyp}^2 = \text{opp}^2 + \text{adj}^2$$

The trig. ratios are used in the following case.

To calculate the length of an unknown side in a right-angled △.

We need to know **at least** one angle (apart from the right-angle) **and** the length of one side.

(Note: If you know 2 sides and have to calculate the third side — use Pythagoras' Theorem.)

Worked Example 3.1

Calculate the length of the unknown side in each of the following △s.
(Round answer off to 1 d.p. where necessary!)

(a)

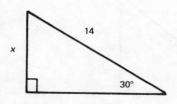

(b)

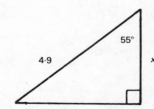

(c)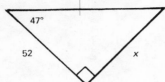

(d)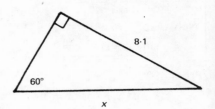

(e)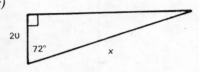

(f)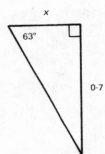

Solutions

Always make a sketch!

(a) SO͟H CA͟H TO͟A

$\sin 30° = \dfrac{\text{opp}}{\text{hyp}}$

$\sin 30° = \dfrac{x}{14}$

$\quad x = 14 \sin 30°$

$\quad = 14 \times 0\cdot5$

$\quad = 7$

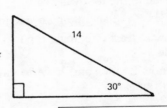

Calculator
Type 14 × 30 sin =

(b) SOH CA͟H TOA

$\cos 55° = \dfrac{\text{adj}}{\text{hyp}}$

$\cos 55° = \dfrac{x}{4\cdot9}$

$\quad x = 4\cdot9 \cos 55°$

$\quad = 2\cdot811 = 2\cdot8 \text{ (to 1 d.p.)}$

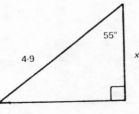

(c) SO̬HCA̬HTO̬A̬

$$\tan 47° = \frac{\text{opp}}{\text{adj}}$$

$$\tan 47° = \frac{x}{52}$$

$$x = 52 \tan 47°$$

$$= 55\!\cdot\!763$$

$$= 55\!\cdot\!8 \text{ (to 1 d.p.)}$$

(d) SO̬HCA̬HTO̬A̬

$$\sin 60° = \frac{\text{opp}}{\text{hyp}}$$

$$\sin 60° = \frac{8\!\cdot\!1}{x}$$

$$x \sin 60° = 8\!\cdot\!1$$

$$x = \frac{8\!\cdot\!1}{\sin 60°}$$

$$x = \frac{8\!\cdot\!1}{\sin 60°}$$

$$= 9\!\cdot\!353$$

$$= 9\!\cdot\!4 \text{ (to 1 d.p.)}$$

Calculator
Type: $8\!\cdot\!1 \div 60 \boxed{\sin} =$

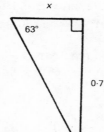

(e) SOHCA̬HTO̬A̬

$$\cos 72° = \frac{\text{adj}}{\text{hyp}}$$

$$\cos 72° = \frac{20}{x}$$

$$x = \frac{20}{\cos 72°}$$

$$= 64\!\cdot\!721$$

$$= 64\!\cdot\!7 \text{ (to 1 d.p.)}$$

(f) SO̬HCA̬HTO̬A̬

$$\tan 63° = \frac{\text{opp}}{\text{adj}}$$

$$\tan 63° = \frac{0\!\cdot\!7}{x}$$

$$x = \frac{0\!\cdot\!7}{\tan 63°}$$

$$= 0\!\cdot\!357$$

$$= 0\!\cdot\!4 \text{ (to 1 d.p.)}$$

Exact Values

It is **important** that you know the following table of exact values.

a	$0°$	$30°$	$45°$	$60°$	$90°$
sin	0	$\frac{1}{2}$	$\frac{1}{\sqrt{2}}$	$\frac{\sqrt{3}}{2}$	1
cos	1	$\frac{\sqrt{3}}{2}$	$\frac{1}{\sqrt{2}}$	$\frac{1}{2}$	0
tan	0	$\frac{1}{\sqrt{3}}$	1	$\sqrt{3}$	$-$

Remember 2 $\triangle$s

$$\sin 30° = \frac{1}{2}$$

$$\boxed{\tan 45° = 1}$$ $$\boxed{1 = \frac{1}{1}}$$

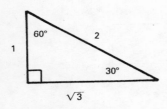

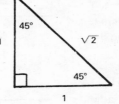

By Pythagoras' Theorem
$2^2 = 1^2 + x^2$
$x^2 = 4 - 1 = 3 \Rightarrow x = \sqrt{3}$

By Pythagoras' Theorem
$x^2 = 1^2 + 1^2 = 1 + 1 = 2 \Rightarrow x = \sqrt{2}$

3.1.2 IMPORTANT FACTS

The following facts (which are 'proven' in Higher Maths) are important.

$\sin a° = \cos (90 - a)°$ $\quad\quad$ $\sin 30° = \cos 60°$
$\cos a° = \sin (90 - a)°$

For example: $\sin 20° = \cos (90 - 20)° = \cos 70°$
$\cos 65° = \sin (90 - 65)° = \sin 25°$

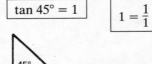

$\sin (-a)° = -\sin a°$
$\cos (-a)° = \cos a°$

For example: $\sin (-30)° = -\sin 30° = -0.5$
$\cos (-60)° = \cos 60° = 0.5$

The 4-quadrants

90

$$\left.\begin{array}{l}\sin +ve \\ \cos \\ \tan\end{array}\right\}-ve \quad \left.\begin{array}{l}\sin \\ \cos \\ \tan\end{array}\right\}+ve$$

180 ———————————— 0   this is abbreviated to $\dfrac{\text{S} \mid \text{A}}{\text{T} \mid \text{C}}$

$$\begin{array}{l}\tan +ve \\ \left.\begin{array}{l}\sin \\ \cos\end{array}\right\}-ve\end{array} \quad \begin{array}{l}\cos +ve \\ \left.\begin{array}{l}\sin \\ \tan\end{array}\right\}-ve\end{array}$$

270

Calculators will confirm these values!

Calculating exact values

1. To calculate sin, cos or tan of any angle between 0° and 90°, i.e. $0 \leqslant a \leqslant 90$, use table of values **or** calculator.

2. To calculate sin, cos or tan of any angle between 90° and 180°, i.e. $90 < a° \leqslant 180$, use the following method (or your **calculator**).

Worked Example 3.2

(a) $\sin 120° = \sin (180 - 60)° = \sin 60°$

$\therefore \sin 120° = \sin 60° = \dfrac{\sqrt{3}}{2}$

(b) $\sin 95° = \sin (180 - 85)° = \sin 85°$ | Calculating an angle in the
$\therefore \sin 95° = \sin 85°$ | 2nd quadrant.

In general $\boxed{\sin (180 - a)° = \sin a°}$

Similarly

$\cos 120° = \cos (180 - 60)° = -\cos 60°$ $\boxed{\text{2nd quadrant } 180 - a}$

$\cos 120° = -\cos 60° = -\dfrac{1}{2}$

$\therefore \boxed{\cos (180 - a)° = -\cos a°}$

and so $\boxed{\tan (180 - a)° = -\tan a°}$

Proof $\tan (180 - a)° = \dfrac{\sin (180 - a)°}{\cos (180 - a)°} = -\dfrac{\sin a°}{\cos a°} = -\tan a°$

3. To calculate sin, cos or tan of any angle between 180° and 270°, i.e. $180 < a \leq 270$, use the following method (or use your calculator!).

Worked Example 3.3

$\sin 210° = \sin (180 + 30)° = -\sin 30°$

$\therefore \sin 210° = -\sin 30° = -0 \cdot 5$

In general $\boxed{\sin (180 + a)° = -\sin a°}$

Similarly

$\cos 210° = \cos (180 + 30)° = -\cos 30°$

$\therefore \cos 210° = -\cos 30° = -\dfrac{\sqrt{3}}{2}$

$\boxed{\text{Calculating an angle in the 3rd quadrant}}$

$\boxed{\cos (180 + a)° = -\cos a°}$

and so $\boxed{\tan (180 + a)° = \tan a°}$ $\boxed{\text{3rd quadrant } 180 + a}$

Proof $\tan (180 + a)° = \dfrac{\sin (180 + a)°}{\cos (180 + a)°} = \dfrac{-\sin a°}{-\cos a°} = \tan a°$

4. To calculate sin, cos or tan of any angle between 270° and 360°, i.e. $270 < a \leq 360$, use the method below (or use your calculator!).

Worked Example 3.4

$\sin 315° = \sin (360 - 45)° = -\sin 45°$

$\therefore \sin 315° = -\sin 45° = -\dfrac{1}{\sqrt{2}}$

In general $\boxed{\sin (360 - a)° = -\sin a°}$

Similarly

$\cos 315° = \cos (360 - 45)° = \cos 45°$

$\therefore \cos 315° = \cos 45° = -\dfrac{1}{\sqrt{2}}$

$\boxed{\text{Calculating an angle in the 4th quadrant}}$

$\therefore \boxed{\cos (360 - a)° = \cos a°}$

and so $\boxed{\tan (360 - a)° = -\tan a°}$ $\boxed{\text{4th quadrant } 360 - a}$

Proof $\tan (360 - a)° = \dfrac{\sin (360 - a)°}{\cos (360 - a)°}$

$= -\dfrac{\sin a°}{\cos a°}$

$= -\tan a°$

3.1.3 BASIC GRAPHS

Graph of $y = \sin x°$

Facts:	maximum value of $\sin x° = 1$
	and minimum value of $\sin x° = -1$

Proof

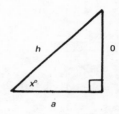

$h = 0^2 + a^2$ since h is the biggest side
then $0 < h$.

$\therefore \sin x° = \dfrac{0}{h} < 1$ because of previous work.

$-1 < \sin x° < 1$

but $\sin 90 = 1$ and $\sin -90 = -1$

$\therefore -1 \leqslant \sin x° \leqslant 1$

Graph

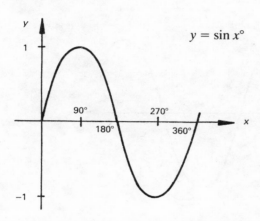

$y = \sin x°$

The sine graph has a **period** of 360°, i.e. every 360° the above shape is repeated.

$y = \sin x°$ has
maximum value of 1
minimum value of -1
period of 360°

Graph of $y = \cos x°$

Facts:	maximum value of $\cos x° = 1$

and minimum value of $\cos x° = -1$

Proof

Since h is the largest side in the $\triangle$ then $a < h$.

$\therefore \cos x° = \dfrac{a}{h} < 1$ because of previous

work on $\dfrac{S}{T} \bigg| \dfrac{A}{C}$

then $-1 < \cos x° < 1$

but $\cos 0° = 1$ and $\cos 180° = -1$

$\therefore -1 \leqslant \cos x° \leqslant 1$

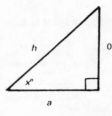

Graph

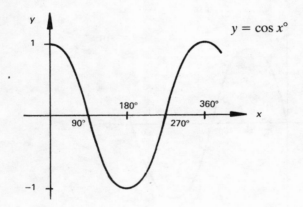

$y = \cos x°$

The cosine graph has a **period** of 360°, i.e. every 360° the above shape is repeated.

$y = \cos x°$ has
maximum value of 1
minimum value of -1
period of 360°

Graph of $y = \tan x°$

Facts:

tan $x°$ has **no** maximum **or** minimum value.

There are however values of x for which tan $x°$ does not exist.

For $x = 90°$, $\tan 90° = \dfrac{\sin 90°}{\cos 90°} = \dfrac{1}{0}$ is undefined, can't divide by 0.

∴ tan $x°$ has no value when cos $x° = 0$

$$\boxed{\cos 90° = \cos 270° = 0}$$

Graph

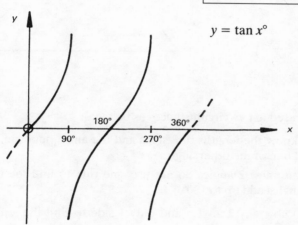

$y = \tan x°$

The tangent graph has a **period** of 180°, i.e. the above graph between 90° and 270° is repeated every 180°.

∴
$y = \tan x°$ has

NO maximum or minimum value
period of 180°

3.1.4   NON-RIGHT-ANGLED △ TRIGONOMETRY

The following rules should **only** be used when the △ under consideration **is not** right-angled. If it is right-angled use 'SOHCAHTOA', i.e. the previous work.

Sine Rule

The sine rule states

$$\frac{a}{\sin A} = \frac{b}{\sin B} = \frac{c}{\sin C}$$

$\left(\text{Alternatively} \right.$

$\left. \frac{\sin A}{a} = \frac{\sin B}{b} = \frac{\sin C}{c} \right)$

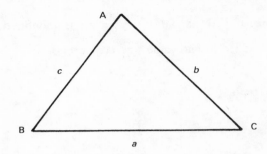

The sine rule is used in **two** circumstances as below:

(i) When you know the lengths of 2 sides **and** the angle opposite one of the sides **to find** one of the other angles.

 (**Note**: If you **know** 2 angles do not use sine rule to find the third angle since **all** 3 angles add up to 180°.)

(ii) When you know **any** 2 angles and only 1 side to find the length of any other side.

Worked Example 3.5

Type (i) example

If in the △ opposite PQ = 5 cm and PR = 6 cm, calculate the sizes of all the angles in △PQR if ∠PQR = 50°.

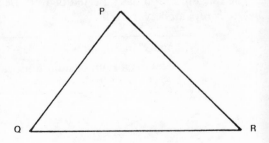

Solution

Draw a sketch!

Using the sine rule

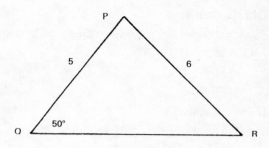

Tick what you know

$$\frac{p}{\sin P} = \frac{q\checkmark}{\sin Q\checkmark} = \frac{r\checkmark}{\sin R}$$

$$\frac{q}{\sin Q} = \frac{r}{\sin R}$$

$$\Leftrightarrow \frac{6}{\sin 50} = \frac{5}{\sin R}$$

$$\Leftrightarrow 6 \sin R = 5 \sin 50$$

$$\Leftrightarrow \sin R = \frac{5 \sin 50}{6} = 0.638$$

$$\therefore R = 39.7° \text{ (to 1 d.p.)}$$

If sin R = 0·638

R = | SHIFT | | SIN | 0·638

Since we now know 2 angles, the 3rd angle is easily found

$$\angle P = 180° - (50 + 39.7)°$$
$$= 180° - 89.7°$$
$$= 90.3°$$

Worked Example 3.6

Type (ii) example

In △FGH, FH = 4·6 mm,
$\angle$F = 70°, $\angle$H = 60°. Find the
length of FG.

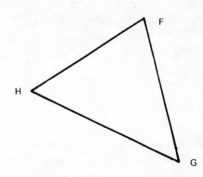

Solution

Draw a sketch!

Since we know 2 of the angles then the third angle, $\angle$ G, is

$$\angle G = 180° - (60 + 70)°$$
$$= 180° - 130°$$
$$= 50°$$

Using the sine rule

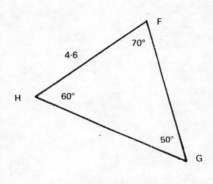

$$\frac{f}{\sin F\checkmark} = \frac{g\checkmark}{\sin G\checkmark} = \frac{h}{\sin H\checkmark}$$

$$\frac{g}{\sin G} = \frac{h}{\sin H}$$

$$\Leftrightarrow \frac{4\cdot6}{\sin 50°} = \frac{h}{\sin 60°}$$

$$\Leftrightarrow h \sin 50° = 4\cdot6 \sin 60°$$

$$\Leftrightarrow \qquad h = \frac{4\cdot6 \sin 60°}{\sin 50°}$$

$$= 5\cdot2 \text{ (to 1 d.p.)}$$

$\therefore$ length of FG is 5·2 mm.

Cosine Rule

The cosine rule states

$$a^2 + b^2 + c^2 - 2bc \cos A \quad\text{——— (1)}$$
$$\left(\begin{array}{l}\text{or } b^2 = a^2 + c^2 - 2ac \cos B \\ \text{or } c^2 = a^2 + b^2 - 2ab \cos C\end{array}\right)$$

or $\cos A \dfrac{b^2 + c^2 - a^2}{2bc} \quad\text{——————— (2)}$

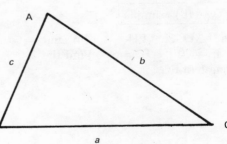

Form (1) of the cosine rule is used when you know the lengths of two sides and **only** the included angle to find the length of the third side.

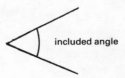

included angle

Form (2) of the cosine rule is used when you know the lengths of all 3 sides and **no** angles to find the size of any angle.

Worked Example 3.7

| Form (1) example |

In $\triangle$KLM opposite,
LM = 14·8 ft, KM = 15·7 ft and
$\angle$ KML = 35°. Find the length of
KL.

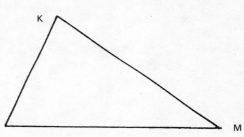

Solution

Draw a sketch!

Since we know 2 sides and the included angle we use form (1) of the cosine rule!

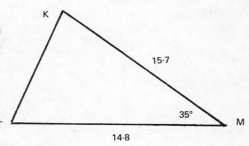

| Calculator steps: 14·8 $\boxed{x^2}$ + 15·7 $\boxed{x^2}$ − (2 × 14·8 × 15·7 × 35 cos) = |

$$\therefore m^2 = k^2 + l^2 - 2kl \cos M$$
$$= (14\text{·}8)^2 + (15\text{·}7)^2 - 2(14\text{·}8)(15\text{·}7) \cos 35°$$
$$= 84\text{·}854$$
$$\therefore m = \sqrt{84\text{·}854}$$
$$= 9\text{·}2 \text{ (to 1 d.p.)}$$
$\therefore$ length of KL is 9·2 ft.

113

Worked Example 3.8

Form (2) example

In the △ opposite calculate the size of ∠ EDF

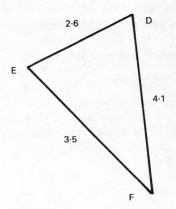

Solution

Draw a sketch!

Since we know 3 sides and no angles and have to calculate an angle — use form (2) of the cosine rule.

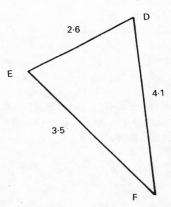

$$\cos D = \frac{e^2 + f^2 - d^2}{2ef}$$

$$= \frac{4 \cdot 1^2 + 2 \cdot 6^2 - 3 \cdot 5^2}{2 \times 4 \cdot 1 \times 2 \cdot 6}$$

$$= 0 \cdot 531$$

$$D = 57 \cdot 9° \text{ (to 1 d.p.)}$$

Calculator steps:
$(4 \cdot 1^2 + 2 \cdot 6^2 - 3 \cdot 5^2) \div (2 \times 4 \cdot 1 \times 2 \cdot 6) =$

Cos D = 0·531

D = | SHIFT | | COS |

Note: Some calculators use | INV | or | 2nd F | instead of | SHIFT |.

Area of a Triangle

For right-angled $\triangle$s or $\triangle$s whose perpendicular height is known.

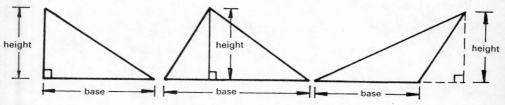

Area of $\triangle = \frac{1}{2} \times$ base $\times$ height

$$A = \frac{1}{2}bh$$

However, if you know 2 sides of any $\triangle$ and the included angle you can also calculate the area.

Area of $\triangle$ABC $= \frac{1}{2}ab \sin C$

or $\frac{1}{2}bc \sin A$

or $\frac{1}{2}ac \sin B$

3.2   RADIAN MEASURE

Angles can be measured in both radians **and** degrees, such that

$180° = \pi$ radians

and π radians $= 180°$.

You must be able to convert between these two modes of measurement.

3.2.1 DEGREES → RADIANS

To convert from degrees to radians **divide by 180 and multiply by** π.

Worked Example 3.9

Convert the following angles measured in degrees into radians.

(a) 60°   *(b)* 150°   *(c)* 270°   *(d)* 330°

Solutions

(a) $60° = \dfrac{60}{180} \times \pi = \dfrac{1}{3}\pi = \dfrac{\pi}{3}$ radians

> Leave the answer in terms of π

(b) $150° = \dfrac{150}{180} \times \pi = \dfrac{5}{6}\pi = \dfrac{5\pi}{6}$ radians

(c) $270° = \dfrac{270}{180} \times \pi = \dfrac{3}{2}\pi = \dfrac{3\pi}{2}$ radians

(d) $330° = \dfrac{330}{180} \times \pi = \dfrac{11}{6}\pi = \dfrac{11\pi}{6}$ radians

3.2.2 RADIANS → DEGREES

To convert from radian measure to degrees **divide by** π **and multiply by 180**
$\left(\text{i.e. multiply by } \dfrac{180}{\pi}\right)$

Worked Example 3.10

Convert the following angles measured in radians into degrees.

(a) $\dfrac{\pi}{4}$ *(b)* $\dfrac{2\pi}{5}$ *(c)* $\dfrac{4\pi}{3}$ *(d)* 7π

Solution

(a) $\dfrac{\pi}{4} = \dfrac{\not\pi}{4} \times \dfrac{180}{\not\pi} = 45°$

(b) $\dfrac{2\pi}{5} = \dfrac{2\pi}{5} \times \dfrac{180}{\pi} = 72°$

116

(c) $\dfrac{4\pi}{3} = \dfrac{4\pi}{3} \times \dfrac{180}{\pi} = 240°$

(d) $7\pi = 7\pi \times \dfrac{180}{\pi} = 1260°$

Most calculators can work in degree or radian mode. Be careful and make sure you are in the correct mode — otherwise you may get strange answers!

3.3   ADDITION FORMULAE

3.3.1   FORMULAE

These are important formulae which should be learned — however they will be given to you in a 'formula list' in the Revised Higher examination.

$$\left.\begin{array}{l} \sin (A + B) = \sin A \cos B + \cos A \sin B \\ \sin (A - B) = \sin A \cos B - \cos A \sin B \end{array}\right\}$$

$$\left.\begin{array}{l} \cos (A + B) = \cos A \cos B - \sin A \sin B \\ \cos (A - B) = \cos A \cos B + \sin A \sin B \end{array}\right\}$$

Worked Example 3.11

Prove that $\sin\left(\theta - \dfrac{\pi}{3}\right) = \dfrac{1}{2}\sin\theta - \dfrac{\sqrt{3}}{2}\cos\theta$.

Solution

$\sin\left(\theta - \dfrac{\pi}{3}\right) = \dfrac{1}{2}\sin\theta - \dfrac{\sqrt{3}}{2}\cos\theta$.

L.H.S. $= \sin\left(\theta - \dfrac{\pi}{3}\right)$ 　　$\boxed{\text{Using formula for } \sin (A - B) \quad A = \theta, B = \dfrac{\pi}{3}}$

$= \sin\theta\cos\dfrac{\pi}{3} - \cos\theta\sin\dfrac{\pi}{3}$

$= \dfrac{1}{2}\sin\theta - \dfrac{\sqrt{3}}{2}\cos\theta$ 　　$\boxed{\cos\dfrac{\pi}{3} = \dfrac{1}{2} \quad \sin\dfrac{\pi}{3} = \dfrac{\sqrt{3}}{2}}$

$= $ R.H.S.

Result proven.

Worked Example 3.12

Find the **exact value** of cos 15°.

Solution

Using the fact that $15° = 45° - 30°$ (**or** $15° = 60° - 45°$!) and the formula for $\cos(A - B)$, then

$$\cos 15° = \cos(45 - 30)°$$
$$= \cos 45° \cos 30° + \sin 45° \sin 30°$$
$$= \frac{1}{\sqrt{2}} \cdot \frac{\sqrt{3}}{2} + \frac{1}{\sqrt{2}} \cdot \frac{1}{2}$$
$$= \frac{\sqrt{3}}{2\sqrt{2}} + \frac{1}{2\sqrt{2}} = \frac{\sqrt{3} + 1}{2\sqrt{2}}$$

(To write this with a **rational denominator** multiply top and bottom by $\sqrt{2}$.)

$$= \frac{\sqrt{2}(\sqrt{3} + 1)}{4}$$

Worked Example 3.13

Show that $3 \sin(x + 60)° - 2 \cos(x - 30)° = \frac{1}{2}(\sin x + \sqrt{3} \cos x)°$.

Solution

$$3 \sin(x + 60)° - 2 \cos(x - 30)° = \frac{1}{2}(\sin x + \sqrt{3} \cos x)°$$

L.H.S. $= 3 \sin(x + 60)° - 2 \cos(x - 30)°$

$$= 3(\sin x \cos 60 + \cos x \sin 60)° - 2(\cos x \cos 30 + \sin x \sin 30)°$$

$$= 3\left(\frac{1}{2}\sin x + \frac{\sqrt{3}}{2}\cos x\right)° - 2\left(\frac{\sqrt{3}}{2}\cos x + \frac{1}{2}\sin x\right)°$$

$$= \frac{3}{2}\sin x° + \frac{3\sqrt{3}}{2}\cos x° - \sqrt{3}\cos x° - \sin x°$$

$$= \frac{3}{2}\sin x° - \sin x° + \frac{3\sqrt{3}}{2}\cos x° - \sqrt{3}\cos x°$$

$$= \frac{1}{2}\sin x° + \frac{\sqrt{3}}{2}\cos x°$$

$$= \frac{1}{2}(\sin x + \sqrt{3}\cos x)°$$

$$= \text{R.H.S.}$$

Worked Example 3.14

If $\sin A = \frac{5}{13}$ and $\cos B = \frac{4}{5}$ (A and B both being acute angles) find the exact value of $\cos (A + B)$.

Solution

(Draw right-angled triangles for A and B!)

Using Pythagoras' Theorem

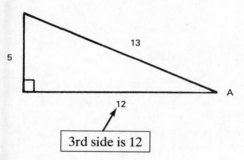

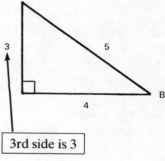

3rd side is 12   3rd side is 3

So $\sin A = \frac{5}{13}$ $\cos B = \frac{4}{5}$

and $\cos A = \frac{12}{13}$ $\sin B = \frac{3}{5}$

$\therefore \cos (A + B) = \cos A \cos B - \sin A \sin B$

$$= \frac{12}{13} \cdot \frac{4}{5} - \frac{5}{13} \cdot \frac{3}{5}$$

$$= \frac{48}{65} - \frac{15}{65}$$

$$= \frac{33}{65}$$

3.4 DOUBLE ANGLE FORMULAE

3.4.1 FORMULAE

These formulae are derived from the formulae given in 3.3.1.

$$\sin 2A = 2 \sin A \cos A$$

Proof $\sin 2A = \sin (A + A)$
$$= \sin A \cos A + \cos A \sin A$$
$$= 2 \sin A \cos A$$

$$\cos 2A = \cos^2 A - \sin^2 A$$
$$= 2 \cos^2 A - 1$$
$$= 1 - 2 \sin^2 A$$

Proof $\cos 2A = \cos (A + A)$
$$= \cos A \cos A - \sin A \sin A$$
$$= \cos^2 A - \sin^2 A$$

| From $\sin^2 A + \cos^2 A = 1$ |

$\sin^2 A = 1 - \cos^2 A$ $\cos^2 A = 1 - \sin^2 A$
$\Rightarrow \cos 2A = \cos^2 A - (1 - \cos^2 A)$ $\cos 2A = 1 - \sin^2 A - \sin^2 A$
            $= 2 \cos^2 A - 1$ $= 1 - 2 \sin^2 A$

Like the formulae given in 3.3.1, it is better if you learn these formulae, however, they are given in the 'formula list'.

Worked Example 3.15

Knowing that $\sin 60° = \dfrac{\sqrt{3}}{2}$ use an appropriate formula to show that $\cos 120° = -\dfrac{1}{2}$.

Solution

$$\cos 120° = \cos(2 \times 60°)$$ | Use cos 2A formula involving sine only |

$\therefore$ Using $\cos 2A = 1 - 2 \sin^2 A$

$$= 1 - 2\left(\frac{\sqrt{3}}{2}\right)^2 \qquad \sin^2 A = (\sin A)^2$$

$$= 1 - 2\left(\frac{3}{4}\right) = 1 - \frac{3}{2} = -\frac{1}{2}$$

$\therefore \cos 120° = -\dfrac{1}{2}$ as required.

Worked Example 3.16

Show that $\dfrac{\sin 2A}{1 + \cos 2A} = \tan A$

Solution

L.H.S. $= \dfrac{\sin 2A}{1 + \cos 2A}$ | We have 2 double angle formulae here. Step 1 — Replace sin 2A by 2 sin A cos A

$= \dfrac{2 \sin A \cos A}{1 + \cos 2A}$

$= \dfrac{2 \sin A \cos A}{1 + 2 \cos^2 A - 1}$ | Step 2 — To eliminate 1 replace cos 2A by $2 \cos^2 A - 1$

$= \dfrac{2 \sin A \cos A}{2 \cos^2 A}$ | 2 and cos A will cancel — note $\cos^2 A$ on denominator

$= \dfrac{\sin A}{\cos A}$

$= \tan A$

$= $ R.H.S.

Hence result proven.

Worked Example 3.17

'Caddy Golf Products' make flags for use on golf courses.

Each flag is made from material in the shape of an isosceles triangle whose dimensions are given below.

If $\angle ABD = \theta° = \angle CBD$

$\qquad AD = 8$ inches

$\qquad AB = 12$ inches

Calculate

(i) sin $A\hat{B}C$

(ii) area of $\triangle ABC$

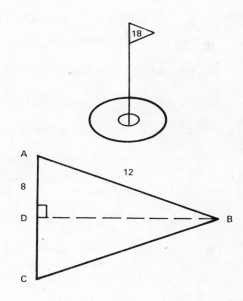

Solution

(i) From △ABD

$$\sin \theta° = \frac{8}{12} = \frac{2}{3}$$

and so $\cos \theta° = \dfrac{4\sqrt{5}}{12} = \dfrac{\sqrt{5}}{3}$

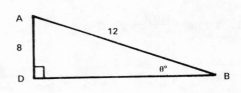

(Calculate BD by
Pythagoras' Theorem.)

∴ since $A\hat{B}C = 2\theta°$

then $\sin A\hat{B}C = \sin 2\theta$

$$= 2 \sin \theta \cos \theta$$

$$= 2 \times \frac{2}{3} \times \frac{\sqrt{5}}{3} = \frac{4\sqrt{5}}{9}$$

(ii) | Method I | — Elementary Arithmetic

Area of △ABC $= \dfrac{1}{2} \times AC \times DB$ $\boxed{\begin{array}{l} AC = 2 \times AD \\ \quad = 2 \times 8 \\ \quad = 16 \end{array}}$

$$= \frac{1}{2} \times 16 \times 4\sqrt{5}$$

$$= 32\sqrt{5} \text{ square inches}$$

| Method II | — Trigonometry

Area of △ABC $= \dfrac{1}{2} \times AB \times BC \times \sin A\hat{B}C$

$$= \frac{1}{2} \times 12 \times 12 \times \frac{4\sqrt{5}}{9}$$

$$= 32\sqrt{5} \text{ square inches.}$$

3.5 TRIGONOMETRICAL GRAPHS

3.5.1 SINE GRAPHS

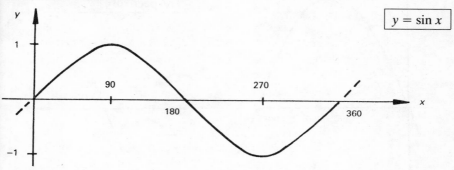

$$y = \sin x$$

<table>
<tr><td>

Reminders
</td><td>

From the graph of $y = \sin x$,
maximum value is 1
minimum value is -1
Period is $360°$ or 2π radians.
</td></tr>
</table>

From this graph, the graph of related functions can be drawn.

$y = a \sin x$

(a) $y = 2 \sin x$

This is the graph of $\sin x$ with same period **but** maximum and minimum values of 2 and -2 respectively.

$$y = 2 \sin x$$

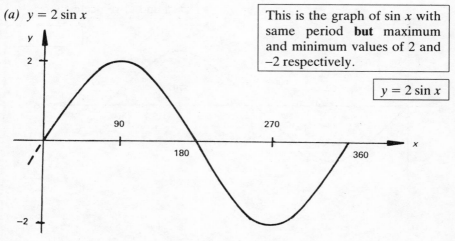

123

(b) $y = 5 \sin x$

> This is the graph of sin x with same period **but** maximum and minimum values of 5 and −5 respectively.

$$y = 5 \sin x$$

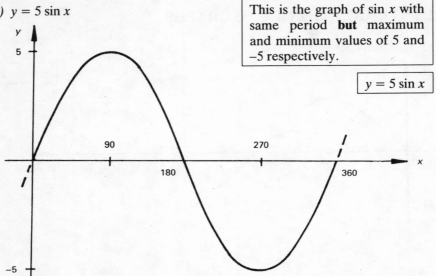

(c) $y = -\sin x$

> This is the graph of sin x reflected in the x-axis. Thus the period is still 360° and maximum and minimum values are 1 and −1 respectively.

$$y = -\sin x$$

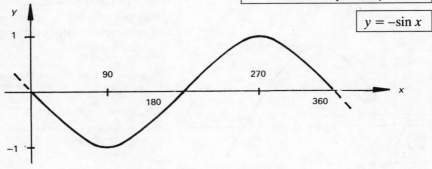

(d) $y = -2 \sin x$

This is the graph of $y = 2 \sin x$ reflected in the x-axis. So period is 360° with maximum and minimum values of 2 and −2 respectively.

$\boxed{y = -2 \sin x}$

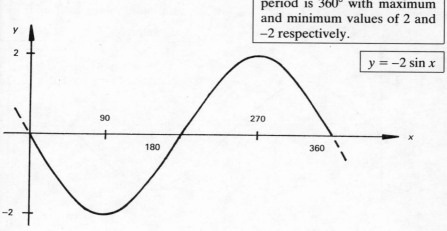

(e) $y = -7 \sin x$

This is the graph of $y = 7 \sin x$ reflected in the x-axis. So period 360° with maximum and minimum values are 7 and −7 respectively.

$\boxed{y = -7 \sin x}$

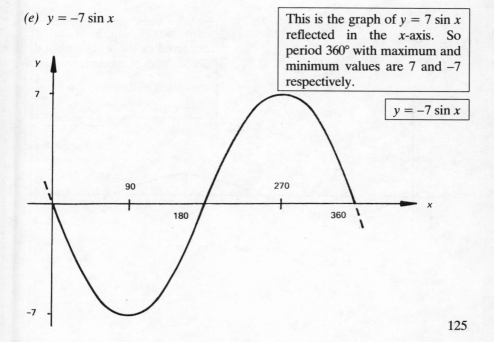

125

(f) $y = \frac{1}{2} \sin x$

This is the graph of sin x with period 360° but maximum and minimum values of $\frac{1}{2}$ and $-\frac{1}{2}$ respectively.

$y = \frac{1}{2} \sin x$

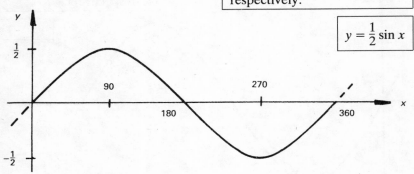

(g) $y = -\frac{1}{5} \sin x$

This is the graph of sin x reflected in the x-axis, period 360° with maximum and minimum values are $\frac{1}{5}$ and $-\frac{1}{5}$ respectively.

$y = -\frac{1}{5} \sin x$

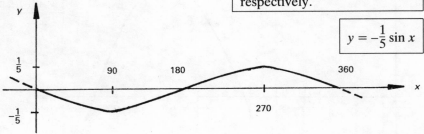

Thus in general, the graph of $y = a \sin x$, $a > 0$, has
— period 360° **or** 2π radians
— maximum and minimum values of a and $-a$ respectively.

$y = \sin ax$

(h) $y = \sin 2x$

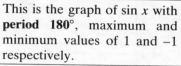

This is the graph of sin x with **period 180°**, maximum and minimum values of 1 and -1 respectively.

$y = \sin 2x$

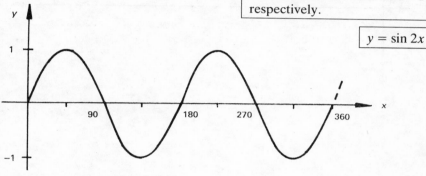

(i) $y = \sin 6x$

This is the graph of sin x with **period 60°**, maximum and minimum values are 1 and -1 respectively.

$y = \sin 6x$

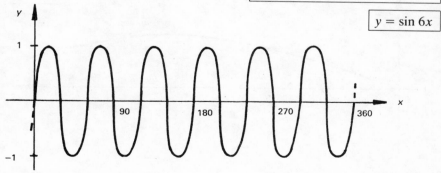

127

(j) $y = \sin \dfrac{x}{2} \left(\text{i.e. } y = \sin \dfrac{1}{2} x \right).$

This is the graph of sin x with **period 720°**, maximum and minimum values of 1 and −1 respectively.

$$y = \sin \dfrac{x}{2}$$

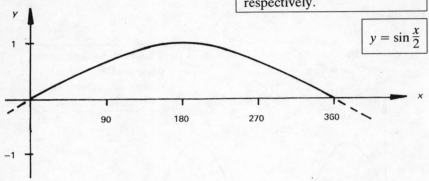

(k) $y = \sin \dfrac{x}{3} \left(\text{i.e. } y = \sin \dfrac{1}{3} x \right).$

This is the graph of sin x with **period 540°**, maximum and minimum values of 1 and −1 respectively.

$$y = \sin \dfrac{x}{3}$$

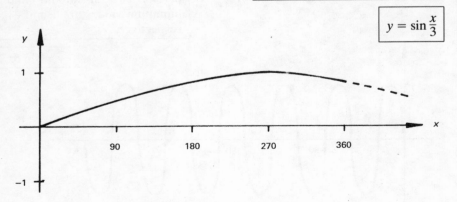

> Thus in general, the graph of $y = \sin ax$ has
> — period $\dfrac{360°}{a}$ or $\dfrac{2\pi}{a}$ radians.
> — maximum and minimum values of 1 and -1 respectively.

$y = a \sin bx$

This section combines both of the previous sections.

(l) $y = 3 \sin 2x$

> This is the graph of $\sin x$ with **period 180°**, maximum and minimum values of 3 and -3 respectively.

> $y = 3 \sin 2x$

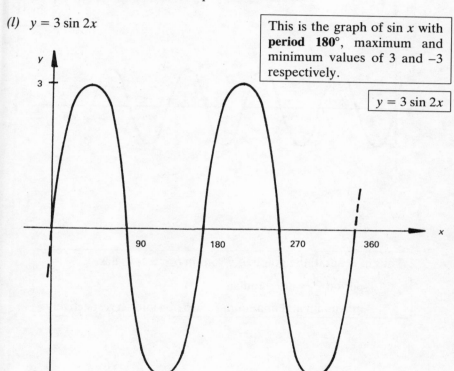

$(m)\ y = -\frac{1}{3}\sin 4x$

> This is the graph of sin x reflected in the x-axis with period 90°, maximum and minimum values of $\frac{1}{3}$ and $-\frac{1}{3}$ respectively.

$$y = -\frac{1}{3}\sin 4x$$

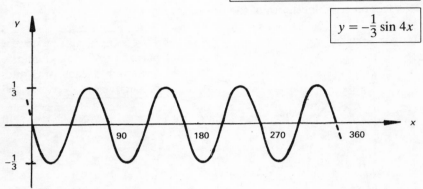

> Thus in general, the graph of $y = a \sin b\,x,\ a > 0$, has
> — period $\dfrac{360°}{b}$ or $\dfrac{2\pi}{b}$ radians.
> — maximum and minimum values of a and $-a$ respectively.

3.5.2   COSINE GRAPHS

The 'rules' learned in (I) apply equally well to the graph of $y = \cos x$ and its related functions as stated below.

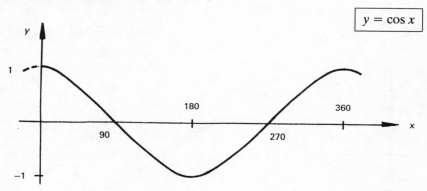

$\boxed{y = \cos x}$

Reminders   From the graph of $y = \cos x$,
　　　　　　　maximum value is 1
　　　　　　　minimum value is -1
　　　　　　　Period is 360° or 2π radians.

$y = a \cos x$, $y = \cos ax$, $y = a \cos bx$

In general

(i) the graph of $y = a \cos x$ has
　　— period 360° or 2π radians,
　　— maximum and minimum values of a and $-a$ respectively.

(ii) the graph of $y = \cos ax$ has
　　— period $\dfrac{360°}{a}$ or $\dfrac{2\pi}{a}$ radians
　　— maximum and minimum values of 1 and -1 respectively.

(iii) the graph of $y = a \cos bx$ has
　　— period $\dfrac{360°}{b}$ or $\dfrac{2\pi}{b}$ radians
　　— maximum and minimum values of a and $-a$ respectively.

Examples

(n) $y = -\frac{1}{3}\cos x$

> This is the graph of cos x reflected in the x-axis with **period 360°**, maximum and minimum values are $\frac{1}{3}$ and $-\frac{1}{3}$ respectively.

$$y = -\frac{1}{3}\cos x$$

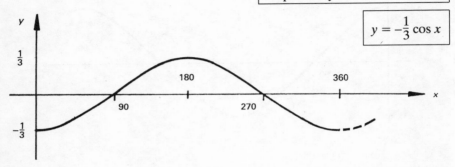

(o) $y = \cos 2x$

> This is the graph of cos x with **period 180°**, maximum and minimum values of 1 and −1 respectively.

$$y = \cos 2x$$

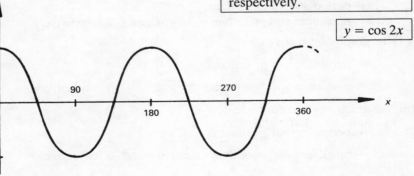

(p) $y = 2 \cos \dfrac{x}{2}$

This is the graph of cos x with **period 720°**, maximum and minimum values of 2 and –2 respectively.

$$y = 2 \cos \frac{x}{2}$$

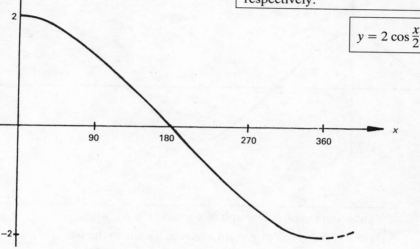

3.5.3 PHASE ANGLES AND OTHER GRAPHS

$y = \sin (x + a)$

(q) $y = \sin (x - 30)°$

This is the graph of sin x moved 30° to the **right**.

$$y = \sin (x - 30)°$$

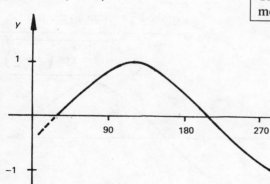

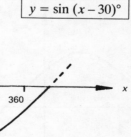

133

(r) $y = \sin (x + 90)°$

This is the graph of sin $x°$ moved 90° to the **left**.

$y = \sin (x + 90)°$

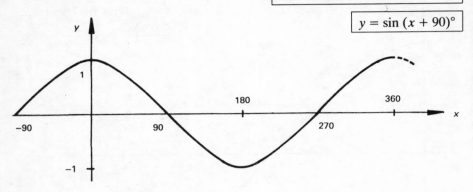

Thus, in general, the graph of $y = \sin (x + a)°$ when

$a > 0$ is the graph of $y = \sin x$ moved a units to the **left**

$a < 0$ is the graph of $y = \sin x$ moved a units to the **right**

The period is still 360° or 2π radians.

The minimum and maximum values are still -1 and 1 respectively.

$y = \cos (x + a)$

(s) $y = \cos \left(x + \dfrac{\pi}{4} \right)$

This is the graph of sin x moved $\dfrac{\pi}{4}$ radians to the **left**.

$y = \cos \left(x + \dfrac{\pi}{4} \right)$

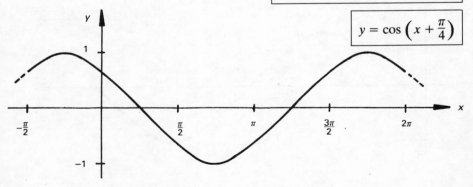

134

(t) $y = \cos(x - 180)°$

This is the graph of sin x moved 180° to the **right**.

$y = \cos(x - 180)°$

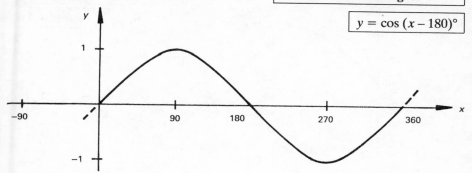

Note this is also the graph of $y = \sin x$.
So $\cos(x - 180) = \sin x$.

Thus, in general, the graph of $y = \cos(x + a)$ when
$a > 0$ is the graph of $y = \cos x$ moved a units to the **left**
$a < 0$ is the graph of $y = \cos x$ moved a units to the **right**
As before, the period is still 360° or 2π radians.
The minimum and maximum values are −1 and 1 respectively.

$y = \sin x + a$, $y = \cos x + a$

When $a > 0$

The graph of $\begin{array}{l} y = \sin x + a \\ y = \cos x + a \end{array}$ is the graph of $\begin{array}{l} \sin x \\ \cos x \end{array}$
moved a units **upwards**.

The period is still 360° or 2π radians.

However, the maximum value is $a + 1$ and the minimum value is $a - 1$.

(u) $y = \sin x° + 3$

> This is the graph of $y = \sin x$ moved **up** 3 units.

$y = \sin x° + 3$

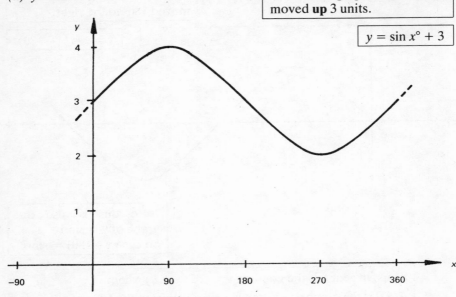

(v) $y = \cos x - 1$

> This is the graph of $y = \cos x$ moved **down** 1 units.

$y = \cos x - 1$

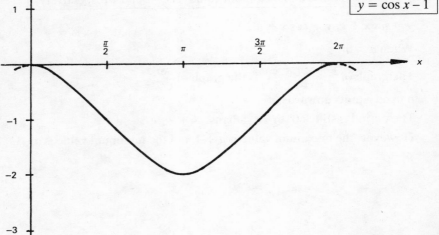

136

3.6 TRIGONOMETRIC EQUATIONS

3.6.1 BASIC TRIGONOMETRIC EQUATIONS

The following examples show all the likely possibilities that may occur in your examination.

Worked Example 3.18

For what values of x, where $0 \leqslant x < 180$, does $3 \sin (2x - 45)°$ have its maximum value?

Solution

Maximum value of
$3 \sin (2x - 45)°$ is 3

since maximum value of
$\sin (2x - 45)° = 1$

Need to solve

$\sin (2x - 45)° = 1 \quad 0 \leqslant x < 180$

$\qquad 2x - 45 = 90 \text{ or } 450 \leftarrow \textbf{too big}!$

$\qquad\qquad 2x = 80 + 45$

$\qquad\qquad x = \dfrac{135}{2} = 67{\cdot}5°$

> Maximum value of
> $\sin (ax + b)$ or $\cos (ax + b)$ is 1
> Minimum value of
> $\sin (ax + b)$ or $\cos (ax + b)$ is -1

> $\sin x = 1$
> $\quad x = 90 \text{ or } 450 \text{ or } \dots$

Worked Example 3.19

Given that $\cos A = \dfrac{1}{5\sqrt{2}}$, where $0 < A < \dfrac{\pi}{2}$, find the **exact** values of

(i) $\sin A$

(ii) $\cos 2A$

(iii) $\sin 2A$

Solution

Draw a right-angled triangle!

By Pythagoras' Theorem

$x^2 + 1^2 = (5\sqrt{2})^2$

$\Rightarrow x^2 + 1 = 50$

$\Rightarrow \quad x^2 = 49$

$\Rightarrow \quad x = \sqrt{49} = 7$ (**Positive** root only since x is the length of a side.)

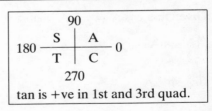

(i) $\sin A = \dfrac{7}{5\sqrt{2}}$

(ii) $\cos 2A = 2\cos^2 A - 1$

Any of the formula may be used
$\cos 2A = 1 - 2\sin^2 A$
$\cos 2A = \cos^2 A - \sin^2 A$

$\qquad\qquad = 2\left(\dfrac{1}{5\sqrt{2}}\right)^2 - 1$

$\qquad\qquad = 2 \times \dfrac{1}{50} - 1$

$\qquad\qquad = \dfrac{1}{25} - 1 = -\dfrac{24}{25}$

(iii) $\sin 2A = 2\sin A \cos A$

$\qquad\qquad = 2\left(\dfrac{7}{5\sqrt{2}}\right)\left(\dfrac{1}{5\sqrt{2}}\right) = \dfrac{14}{50} = \dfrac{7}{25}$

Worked Example 3.20

Solve $2\tan 3\theta - 1 = 0$ for $0 \leqslant \theta < 360°$

Solution

$2\tan 3\theta - 1 = 0$ $0 \leqslant \theta < 360$

$\Rightarrow \quad 2\tan 3\theta = 1$ $\therefore 0 \leqslant 3\theta < 1080$

Rearrange to obtain $\tan 3\theta = \ldots$

$\Rightarrow \qquad \tan 3\theta = \dfrac{1}{2}$ Let $3\theta = a$

$\Rightarrow \qquad \tan a = \dfrac{1}{2}$ $0 \leqslant a < 1080$

$\Rightarrow \qquad\quad a = 26\cdot57 \text{ or } 206\cdot57$
$\qquad\qquad\qquad \text{or } 386\cdot57 \text{ or } 566\cdot57$
$\qquad\qquad\qquad \text{or } 746\cdot57 \text{ or } 926\cdot57$

$\Rightarrow \qquad\quad 3\theta = 26\cdot57 \text{ or } 206\cdot57$
$\qquad\qquad\qquad \text{or } 386\cdot57 \text{ or } 566\cdot57$
$\qquad\qquad\qquad \text{or } 746\cdot57 \text{ or } 926\cdot57$

$\Rightarrow \qquad\quad \theta = 8\cdot9 \text{ or } 68\cdot9 \text{ or } 128\cdot9$
$\qquad\qquad\qquad \text{or } 188\cdot9 \text{ or } 248\cdot9 \text{ or } 308\cdot9$

```
          90
      S  |  A
180 -----+----- 0
      T  |  C
         270
tan is +ve in 1st and 3rd quad.
```

You must ensure that you obtain **all** solutions!

Worked Example 3.21

Solve $\quad 3 \sin^2 x = \frac{1}{3}$ for $0 < x < 270$

Solution

$$3 \sin^2 x = \frac{1}{3}$$

$\Rightarrow \quad \sin^2 x = \frac{1}{9}$

> Need to take +ve and −ve square root.

$\Rightarrow \quad \sin x = \pm \frac{1}{3}$

Solving

$\sin x = \frac{1}{3} \qquad 0 < x < 270$

```
            90
        S  │  A
  180 ──────┼────── 0
        T  │  C
           270
```

$\Rightarrow \quad x = 19 \cdot 47°$ or $160 \cdot 532°$

and

sin +ve in 1st and 2nd quadrant

$\sin x = -\frac{1}{3}$

> Need only −ve solution in **3rd** quadrant

$\Rightarrow \quad x = 199 \cdot 47$

Solution is $x = 19 \cdot 5$ or $160 \cdot 5$ or $199 \cdot 5$ (to 1 d.p.)

> Note: Try to give the answer in the same measurements
> as the question, i.e. if degrees, try to keep as
> degrees, if radians, try to keep as radians.

Worked Example 3.22

Solve $\quad 2 \cos^2 \left(\theta - \frac{\pi}{2} \right) - 2 = 0 \qquad 0 \leqslant \theta < \pi$

Solution

$$2 \cos^2 \left(\theta - \frac{\pi}{2} \right) - 2 = 0$$

$\Rightarrow 2 \cos^2 \left(\theta - \frac{\pi}{2} \right) = 2$

$\Rightarrow \quad \cos^2 \left(\theta - \frac{\pi}{2} \right) = 1$

> Again +ve and −ve square root

$\Rightarrow \quad \cos \left(\theta - \frac{\pi}{2} \right) = \pm 1$

139

Solving for $0 \leqslant \theta < \pi$

$\cos\left(\theta - \dfrac{\pi}{2}\right) = 1$ and $\cos\left(\theta - \dfrac{\pi}{2}\right) = -1$

$\qquad\quad \theta - \dfrac{\pi}{2} = 0$ $\qquad\qquad\quad \theta - \dfrac{\pi}{2} = -\pi \text{ or } \pi$

$\qquad\qquad\quad \theta = \dfrac{\pi}{2}$ $\qquad\qquad\qquad \theta = -\dfrac{\pi}{2} \text{ or } \dfrac{3\pi}{2}$

$\qquad\qquad\qquad\qquad\qquad\qquad\qquad$ No solution in given domain.

$\therefore$ Solution is $x = \dfrac{\pi}{2}$.

> You must take careful note of the range of values allowed in the solution!

Worked Example 3.23

Solve $\quad \cos 2x = 1 - 3\cos x$ for $0 \leqslant x < 2\pi$

Solution

> In the majority of trigonometric equations involving cos $2x$ **and** sin x **or** cos x a quadratic equation is formed.
>
> If **cos $2x$** and **cos x** form and solve an equation of the form $a\cos^2 x + b\cos x + c = 0$ (replace cos $2x$ by $2\cos^2 x - 1$).
>
> If **cos $2x$** and **sin x** form and solve an equation of the form $a\sin^2 x + b\sin x + c = 0$ (replace cos $2x$ by $1 - 2\sin^2 x$).

$\qquad \cos 2x = 1 - 3\cos x$ $\boxed{\text{Replace cos } 2x \text{ by } 2\cos^2 x - 1}$

$\Rightarrow 2\cos^2 x - 1 = 1 - 3\cos x$

$\Rightarrow 2\cos^2 x + 3\cos x - 2 = 0$ $\boxed{\text{Quadratic in cos } x}$

$\Rightarrow (2\cos x - 1)(\cos x + 2) = 0$

$\Rightarrow 2\cos x - 1 = 0 \text{ or } \cos x + 2 = 0$ $\boxed{2x^2 + 3x - 2 = (2x-1)(x+2)}$

$\Rightarrow \cos x = \dfrac{1}{2} \text{ or } \qquad \cos x = -2$ $\boxed{\text{No solution since } -1 \leqslant \cos x \leqslant 1}$

$\therefore$ Solving $\cos x = \dfrac{1}{2}$ $\quad 0 \leqslant x < 2\pi$

$\qquad\qquad\qquad x = \dfrac{\pi}{3} \text{ or } \dfrac{5\pi}{3}$

Worked Example 3.24

Solve $2\cos 2x - 3\sin x = 1$ for $0 \leqslant x < 360$

Solution

$2\cos 2x - 3\sin x = 1$

	Replace $\cos 2x$ by $1 - 2\sin^2 x$ and form quadratic in $\sin x$.

$\Rightarrow 2(1 - 2\sin^2 x) - 3\sin x = 1$

$\Rightarrow 2 - 4\sin^2 x - 3\sin x = 1$

$\Rightarrow 4\sin^2 x + 3\sin x - 1 = 0$

$\Rightarrow (\sin x + 1)(4\sin x - 1) = 0$

$$4x^2 + 3x - 1 = 0$$
$$(x + 1)(4x - 1) = 0$$

$\Rightarrow \sin x + 1 = 0$ or $4\sin x - 1 = 0$

$\Rightarrow \sin x = -1$ or $\sin x = \dfrac{1}{4}$

$\therefore$ Solving $\sin x = -1$ for $0 \leqslant x < 360$

$\qquad\qquad x = 270$

and $\sin x = \dfrac{1}{4}$ for $0 \leqslant x < 360$

$\qquad\qquad x = 14 \cdot 5$ or $165 \cdot 5$

$\therefore$ Solutions are $x = 14 \cdot 5°$ or $165 \cdot 5°$ or $270°$

3.6.2   WAVE EQUATIONS

Any equation of the form
$$a\cos x + b\sin x$$
can be written in one of the four forms

$\qquad\qquad k\cos(x + \alpha)$

$\qquad$ or $\quad k\cos(x - \alpha)$

$\qquad$ or $\quad k\sin(x + \alpha)$

$\qquad$ or $\quad k\sin(x - \alpha)$

In each of these
$k = a^2 + b^2$
$\tan \alpha = \dfrac{b}{a}$

The format to use will usually be given in the examination and the worked examples on the following pages show how to transform any equation of the form $a\cos x + b\sin x$.

Worked Example 3.25

Express $\sqrt{2}\cos x° - \sin x°$ in the form $k\cos(x + \alpha)°$
where $k > 0$ and $0 < \alpha < 360$
Hence find the values of k and α.

Solution

$$\sqrt{2}\cos x° - \sin x° = k\cos(x + \alpha)$$
$$\Rightarrow \sqrt{2}\cos x° - \sin x° = k\cos x\cos\alpha - k\sin x\sin\alpha$$
$$\Rightarrow k\cos\alpha = \sqrt{2} \Rightarrow k^2\cos^2\alpha = 2 \quad \boxed{\text{Equating coefficients}}$$
$$k\sin\alpha = 1 \Rightarrow k^2\sin^2\alpha = 1$$
$$k^2\cos^2\alpha + k^2\sin^2\alpha = 3$$
$$k^2(\cos^2\alpha + k^2\sin^2\alpha) = 3 \quad \boxed{\cos^2\theta + \sin^2\theta = 1}$$
$$k^2 = 3$$
$$k = \sqrt{3}$$

$$\boxed{\begin{array}{l} \textbf{Quick Method} \\ a = \sqrt{2} \quad b = -1 \\ k^2 = a^2 + b^2 = 2 + 1 = 3 \\ k = \sqrt{3} \end{array}}$$

$$\frac{k\sin\alpha}{k\cos\alpha} = \frac{1}{\sqrt{2}} \quad \boxed{\begin{array}{l} \text{since } \sin\alpha > 0 \text{ and } \cos\alpha > 0 \\ \Leftrightarrow \alpha \text{ is in 1st quadrant} \end{array}}$$

$$\Rightarrow \tan\alpha = \frac{1}{\sqrt{2}}$$
$$\alpha = 45°$$
$$\therefore \sqrt{2}\cos x - \sin x = \sqrt{3}\cos(x + 45)°$$

Worked Example 3.26

Express $10\cos 20t + 15\sin 20t$ in the form $R\sin(20t + \alpha)$ where $R > 0$ and $0 \leq \alpha < 360$.

Solution

$$10 \cos 20t + 15 \sin 20t = R \sin (20t + \alpha)$$
$$\Rightarrow 10 \cos 20t + 15 \sin 20t = R \sin 20t \cos \alpha + R \cos 20t \sin \alpha$$

$\Rightarrow \left. \begin{array}{l} R \cos \alpha = 15 \\ R \sin \alpha = 10 \end{array} \right\} \Rightarrow R^2 = 15^2 + 10^2$ | Equating coefficients |

$$= 225 + 100$$
$$= 325$$
$$\therefore R = \sqrt{325} = \sqrt{25 \times 13}$$
$$= 5\sqrt{13}$$

$\dfrac{R \sin \alpha}{R \cos \alpha} = \tan \alpha = \dfrac{10}{15} = \dfrac{2}{3}$ | $\sin \alpha > 0$ and $\cos \alpha > 0$ so α is in 1st quadrant. |

$$\therefore \alpha = 33\cdot7$$
$$\therefore 10 \cos 20t + 15 \sin 20t = 5\sqrt{13} \sin (20t + 33\cdot7).$$

Worked Example 3.27

In an experimental ship tank, the expression $25 \sin 10t - 50 \cos 10t$ is used to represent the displacement of a wave after t seconds. It is found that this expression can be written in the form $k \sin (10t - \alpha)$ where $k > 0$ and $0 \leqslant \alpha \leqslant 360$.

(a) Find the values of k and α.

(b) What is the amplitude of the wave?

Solution

(a) $25 \sin 10t - 50 \cos 10t = k \sin (10t - \alpha)$
$$\Rightarrow 25 \sin 10t - 50 \cos 10t = k \sin 10t \cos \alpha - k \cos 10t \sin \alpha$$

$\Rightarrow \left. \begin{array}{l} k \cos \alpha = 25 \\ k \sin \alpha = 50 \end{array} \right\} \Rightarrow k^2 = 25^2 + 50^2$ | Equating coefficients |

$$= 625 + 2500$$
$$= 3125$$
$$\Rightarrow k = \sqrt{3125} = \sqrt{625 \times 5}$$
$$= 25\sqrt{5}$$

$\dfrac{k \sin \alpha}{k \cos \alpha} = \tan \alpha = \dfrac{10}{25} = 2$ | $\sin \alpha > 0$ and $\cos \alpha > 0$ so α is in 1st quadrant. |

$$\therefore \alpha = 63\cdot4$$
$$\therefore 25 \sin 10t - 50 \cos 10t = 25\sqrt{5} \sin (10t - 63\cdot4)$$

(b) Amplitude = $k = 25\sqrt{5}$.

Worked Example 3.28

Express $6 \sin 100x - \cos 100x$ in the form $R \cos (100x - \alpha)$
where $R > 0$ and $0 \leqslant \alpha < 360$

Solution

$$6 \sin 100x - 8 \cos 100x = R \cos (100x - \alpha)$$

$$\Rightarrow \underline{6} \sin 100x - \underline{8} \cos 100x = \underline{R} \cos 100x \, \underline{\cos \alpha} + \underline{R} \sin 100x \, \underline{\sin \alpha}$$

Note sign!!!

$$\Rightarrow \left. \begin{array}{l} R \cos \alpha = -8 \\ R \sin \alpha = 6 \end{array} \right\} \Rightarrow R^2 = (-8)^2 + 6^2 \qquad \boxed{\text{Equating coefficients}}$$

$$= 64 + 36$$

$$= 100$$

$$\Rightarrow R = \sqrt{100} = 10$$

$$\frac{R \sin \alpha}{R \cos \alpha} = \frac{6}{-8} = -\frac{3}{4} \qquad \boxed{\begin{array}{l} \text{Since } \sin \alpha > 0 \text{ and } \cos \alpha < 0 \text{ so} \\ \alpha \text{ is in 2nd quadrant.} \end{array}}$$

$$\therefore \tan \alpha = -\frac{3}{4}$$

$$\therefore \alpha = 143 \cdot 1$$

so $6 \sin 100x - 8 \cos 100x = 10 \cos (100x - 143 \cdot 1)$

CALCULUS SECTION 4

4.1 DIFFERENTIAL CALCULUS

4.2 INTEGRAL CALCULUS

4.1 DIFFERENTIAL CALCULUS

4.1.1 INTRODUCTION AND NOTATION

Differential calculus or differentiation is used to determine the rate of change of one quantity with respect to another related quantity.

Thus if f is a function of x, i.e. $f(x)$ then the rate of change of f with respect to x is called the derivative of f written as $f'(x)$ (read f dashed x).

Similarly if g is a function of u, i.e. $g(u)$ then the derivative is written as $g'(u)$.

Also, if y is a function of x such that y = expression in x then the derivative is written as $\dfrac{dy}{dx}$.

If h is a function of θ such that y = expression in θ then the derivative is written as $\dfrac{dh}{d\theta}$.

These last two examples, $\dfrac{dy}{dx}$ and $\dfrac{dh}{d\theta}$, show Leibnitz notation for the derivative.

Given any function, say $f(x)$, the derivative (or derived function) can be found by using 'first principles' where

$$f'(x) = \lim_{h \to 0} \frac{f(x + h) - f(x)}{h}$$

Worked Example 4.1

Using first principles find the derivate of

(i) $f(x) = x^2$ (ii) $f(x) = \dfrac{1}{x}$

Solution

(i) Since $f(x) = x^2$ then $f(x + h) = (x + h)^2$

and so $f'(x) = \lim\limits_{h \to 0} \dfrac{f(x + h) - f(x)}{h}$

$= \lim\limits_{h \to 0} \dfrac{(x + h)^2 - x^2}{h}$

$= \lim\limits_{h \to 0} \dfrac{\cancel{x^2} + 2xh + h^2 - \cancel{x^2}}{h}$

$= \lim\limits_{h \to 0} \dfrac{2xh + h^2}{h}$

$= \lim\limits_{h \to 0} \dfrac{\cancel{h}(2x + h)}{\cancel{h}}$

$= \lim\limits_{h \to 0} 2x + h$

$= 2x$

Thus if $f(x) = x^2$ then $f'(x) = 2x$.

By using this method we have **proved** that the derivative of x^2 is $2x$.

(ii) Since $f(x) = \dfrac{1}{x}$ then $f(x + h) = \dfrac{1}{x + h}$

and so $f'(x) = \lim\limits_{h \to 0} \dfrac{f(x + h) - f(x)}{h}$

$= \lim\limits_{h \to 0} \dfrac{1}{h}\left(\dfrac{1}{x + h} - \dfrac{1}{x}\right)$

$= \lim\limits_{h \to 0} \dfrac{1}{h}\left(\dfrac{x}{x(x + h)} - \dfrac{x + h}{x(x + h)}\right)$

$= \lim\limits_{h \to 0} \dfrac{1}{h}\left(\dfrac{x - (x + h)}{x(x + h)}\right)$

$= \lim\limits_{h \to 0} \dfrac{1}{h}\left(\dfrac{x - x - h}{x(x + h)}\right)$

$= \lim\limits_{h \to 0} \dfrac{1}{\cancel{h}}\left(\dfrac{-\cancel{h}}{x + h}\right)$

$= \lim\limits_{h \to 0} \left(\dfrac{-1}{x(x + h)}\right)$

$= -\dfrac{1}{x^2}$

Thus if $f(x) = \dfrac{1}{x}$ then $f'(x) = -\dfrac{1}{x^2}$

Again by using the method of first principles we have proved that the derivative of $\frac{1}{x}$ is $-\frac{1}{x^2}$.

You **will not** be asked to prove the derivative of any function by means of first principles in the Revised Higher examination.

4.1.2 BASIC RULES

It is both time consuming and tedious to find a derivative using first principles — derivatives can be found quicker by using a set of standard rules.

The most commonly used rules are given below:

$$\text{(I)} \quad f(x) = x^n \Rightarrow f'(x) = nx^{n-1}, x \in \mathbf{R}$$

Worked Example 4.2

(a) $f(x) = x^4 \Rightarrow f'(x) = 4x^3$ $\boxed{\text{Here } n = 4}$

(b) $f(x) = x^{-3} \Rightarrow f'(x) = -3x^{-4}$ $\boxed{-3 - 1 = -4}$

(c) $f(x) = \sqrt[3]{x} = x^{1/3}$ $\boxed{\text{Remember } \sqrt[a]{x} = x^{1/a}}$

$$\Rightarrow f'(x) = \frac{1}{3}x^{1/3 - 1} = \frac{1}{3}x^{-2/3} \qquad \sqrt[3]{x} = x^{1/3}$$

(d) $f(x) = \frac{1}{x^2} = x^{-2}$ $\boxed{\text{Remember } \frac{1}{x^a} = x^{-a}}$

$$\Rightarrow f'(x) = -2x^{-3}\left(= -\frac{2}{x^3}\right) \qquad \frac{1}{x^2} = x^{-2}$$

(e) $f(x) = x^{3/5} \Rightarrow f'(x) = \frac{3}{5}x^{3/5 - 1} = \frac{3}{5}^{-2/5}$

(f) $\quad f(x) = \frac{1}{x^{7/4}} = x^{-7/4}$

$$\Rightarrow f'(x) = -\frac{7}{4}x^{-7/4 - 1} = -\frac{7}{4}x^{-11/4}\left(= -\frac{7}{4x^{11/4}}\right)$$

(II) $f(x) = kx^n \Rightarrow f'(x) = knx^{n-1}, n \in \mathbf{R}$ k is a constant.

Worked Example 4.3

(a) $f(x) = 5x^2 \Rightarrow f'(x) = 5 \cdot 2x = 10x$

(b) $g(u) = 6\sqrt{u} = 6u^{1/2} \Rightarrow g'(u) = 6 \cdot \frac{1}{2}u^{-1/2} = 3u^{-1/2}$

$$\boxed{\begin{array}{l} \text{Remember } \sqrt{a} = a^{1/2} \\ \text{so } \sqrt{u} = u^{1/2} \end{array}} \quad \left(= \frac{3}{u^{1/2}} = \frac{3}{\sqrt{u}} \right)$$

(c) $h(t) = \frac{1}{4t^2} = \frac{1}{4} \cdot \frac{1}{t^2} = \frac{1}{4}t^{-2}$ $\boxed{\begin{array}{l} \text{N.B. } \dfrac{1}{4t^2} \neq 4t^{-2} \\[2mm] \dfrac{1}{4t^2} = \dfrac{1}{4}t^{-2} \end{array}}$

$\Rightarrow h'(t) = \frac{1}{4} \cdot (-2t^{-3})$

$\qquad = -\frac{1}{2}t^{-3} \left(= -\frac{1}{2t^3} \right)$

(d) $f(x) = \frac{5}{8}x^4 \Rightarrow f'(x) = \frac{5}{8}(4x^3) = \frac{5}{2}x^3$

(e) $f(x) = -\frac{7}{9x^3}$

$\qquad = -\frac{7}{9} \cdot \frac{1}{x^3} = -\frac{7}{9}x^{-3}$

$\Rightarrow f'(x) = -\frac{7}{9}(-3x^{-4}) = \frac{7}{3}x^{-4} \left(= \frac{7}{3x^4} \right)$

Note that:

(i) $f(x) = x \Rightarrow f'(x) = 1$

(ii) $f(x) = kx \Rightarrow f'(x) = k$, k is a constant.

(iii) $f(x) = 1 \Rightarrow f'(x) = 0$

(iv) $f(x) = k \Rightarrow f'(x) = 0$, k is a constant.

(III) $f(x) = g(x) + h(x) + k(x)$

           $\Rightarrow f'(x) = g'(x) + h'(x) + k'(x)$

This rule is best shown by means of examples.

Worked Example 4.4

(a) $f(x) = x^4 + 3x - 5$ | Find the derivative of each term,

       $\Rightarrow f'(x) = 4x^3 + 3$ | i.e. x^4, $3x$ and -5

Note: we are simply using rules (I) and (II)

(b) $f(x) = 5\sqrt{x} - 9x^4 + x^{16/3} = 5x^{1/2} - 9x^4 + x^{16/3}$

     $\Rightarrow f'(x) = \dfrac{5}{2}x^{-1/2} - 36x^3 + \dfrac{16}{3}x^{13/3}$

(c) $f(x) = x^2\left(x^5 - x^{1/4} - \dfrac{1}{x^3}\right)$ | Here we must expand bracket and simplify **before** evaluating derivative.

        $= x^7 - x^{9/4} - x^{-1}$ | Remember $x^a \cdot x^b = x^{a+b}$

     $\Rightarrow f'(x) = 7x^6 - \dfrac{9}{4}x^{5/4} + x^{-2}$ | $\dfrac{x^a}{x^b} = x^a \div x^b = x^{a-b}$

(d) $f(x) = (x + 4)(x - 5)$ | Again expand and simplify

       $= x^2 - x - 20$

    $f'(x) = 2x - 1$

(e) $f(x) \, (x + 2)(2x - 1)(x + 3)$

        $= 2x^3 + 9x^2 + 7x - 6$

     $\Rightarrow f'(x) = 6x^2 + 18x + 7$

(f) $f(x) = \dfrac{6x + 5}{x}$ | Here we must split the fraction into parts

      $= \dfrac{6x}{x} + \dfrac{5}{x}$ | Now simplify

      $= 6 + \dfrac{5}{x} = 6 + 5x^{-1}$ | Now we can differentiate

    $\Rightarrow f'(x) = -5x^{-2}\left(= -\dfrac{5}{x^2}\right)$

(g) $f(x) = \dfrac{3x^2 + 7x^{1/3}}{x}$

$\boxed{\textbf{Same steps as page 150!}}$

$= \dfrac{3x^2}{x} + \dfrac{7x^{1/3}}{x}$

$= 3x + 7x^{-2/3}$

$\Rightarrow f'(x) = 3 - \dfrac{14}{3}x^{-5/3}$

$\boxed{\begin{array}{l}\text{Remember } \dfrac{x^a}{x^b} = x^{a-b} \\[2mm] \quad \dfrac{x^{1/3}}{x} = \dfrac{x^{1/3}}{x^1} = x^{1/3-1} = x^{-2/3}\end{array}}$

(h) $g(x) = \dfrac{x^{3/2} + x^4}{2\sqrt{x}}$

$\boxed{\text{Remember } \sqrt{x} = x^{1/2}}$

$= \dfrac{x^{3/2}}{2\sqrt{x}} + \dfrac{x^4}{2\sqrt{x}} = \dfrac{x^{3/2}}{2x^{1/2}} + \dfrac{x^4}{2x^{1/2}}$

$= \dfrac{1}{2}x^1 + \dfrac{1}{2}x^{7/2}$

$\Rightarrow g'(x) = \dfrac{1}{2} + \dfrac{7}{4}x^{5/2}$

$\boxed{\begin{array}{l}\dfrac{x^{3/2}}{2x^{1/2}} \\[3mm] = \dfrac{1}{2} \cdot \dfrac{x^{3/2}}{x^{1/2}} = \dfrac{1}{2}x^1\end{array}}$

(i) $h(x) = \dfrac{6x^{3/5} - 5x^{1/2}}{2x^{2/5}}$

$= \dfrac{6x^{3/5}}{2x^{2/5}} - \dfrac{5x^{1/2}}{2x^{2/5}}$

$= 3x^{1/5} - \dfrac{5}{2}x^{1/10}$

$\boxed{\begin{array}{l}\dfrac{x^{1/2}}{x^{2/5}} \\[2mm] = x^{1/2 - 2/5} \\[2mm] = x^{\frac{5-4}{10}} = x^{1/10}\end{array}}$

$\Rightarrow h'(x) = \dfrac{3}{5}x^{-4/5} - \dfrac{1}{4}x^{-9/10}$

$\boxed{\dfrac{1\cancel{5}}{2} \cdot \dfrac{1}{\cancel{10}_2} = \dfrac{1}{4}}$

4.1.3 TANGENTS TO A CURVE

Geometrically, the derivative gives the gradient of the tangent to a curve.

The tangent at a point (x_1, y_1) on a curve, is a **straight line** which **only** meets the curve at the point (x_1, y_1).

The gradient of the tangent, $m_{tangent}$, is given by:

$$m_{tangent} = f'(x) \text{ at } x = x_1$$
$$= f'(x_1)$$

Since the tangent is a straight line its equation can be found by using

$$y - y_1 = m(x - x_1) \text{ where } m = f'(x_1)$$

Worked Example 4.5

Find the equation of the tangent to the curve $f(x) = 5x^4 + 1$ at the point $(1, 6)$.

Solution

> Here we know the equation of the curve **and** the point of contact of tangent and curve. We need only calculate the gradient of the tangent, i.e. $f'(x)$ at $x = 1$, i.e. $f'(1)$ and use $y - y_1 = m(x - x_1)$ to determine equation.

$$m_{tangent} = f'(x) \text{ at } x = 1$$

When $f(x) = 5x^4 + 1 \Rightarrow f'(x) = 20x^3$

$\therefore m_{tangent} = f'(1) = 20.1^3 = 20$

$\therefore$ Equation of tangent using

$$y - y_1 = m(x - x_1) \text{ with } \begin{matrix} m = 20 \\ (x_1, y_1) = (1, 6) \end{matrix}$$

is

$$y - 6 = 20(x - 1)$$
$$\Rightarrow y - 6 = 20x - 20$$
$$\Rightarrow 20x - y - 14 = 0 \text{ (\textbf{or} } y = 20x - 14 \text{ \textbf{or} } y - 20x + 14 = 0)$$

Worked Example 4.6

Find the equation of the tangent to the curve $y = \dfrac{2}{3x}$ at the point where $x = 4$.

Solution

> Here we only have the equation of the curve and the value of the x co-ordinate where the tangent and curve meet.
>
> To determine the equation of the tangent, we must calculate both the y co-ordinate and the gradient of the tangent.

Given $y = \dfrac{2}{3x}$

when $x = 4$, $y = \dfrac{2}{3 \times 4} = \dfrac{1}{6}$

$\therefore$ point of contact is $\left(4, \dfrac{1}{6}\right)$

and $m_{\text{tangent}} = \dfrac{dy}{dx}$ at $x = 4$ 〔 Note notation! 〕

$\therefore \dfrac{dy}{dx} = -\dfrac{2}{3}x^{-2} = -\dfrac{2}{3x^2}$

$$\boxed{\begin{aligned} y &= \frac{2}{3x} \\ &= \frac{2}{3}x^{-1} \\ \therefore \frac{dy}{dx} &= -\frac{2}{3}x^{-2} \end{aligned}}$$

$\therefore m_{\text{tangent}} = -\dfrac{2}{3(4^2)} = -\dfrac{1}{24}$

So using $y - y_1 = m(x - x_1)$ with $\quad m = -\dfrac{1}{24}$

$$(x_1, y_1) = \left(4, \dfrac{1}{6}\right)$$

the equation of the tangent is

$y - \dfrac{1}{6} = -\dfrac{1}{24}(x - 4)$

〔 Multiply through by 24 to eliminate fractions 〕

$24\left(y - \dfrac{1}{6}\right) = -(x - 4)$

$24y - 4 = -x + 4$

$x + 24y - 8 = 0$ (**or** $x + 24y = 8$ **or** $24y = 8 - x$)

$$\boxed{\begin{aligned} &-(x - 4) \\ &= -x - (-4) \\ &= -x + 4 \end{aligned}}$$

Worked Example 4.7

Calculate the angle between the x-axis and the tangent at the point $(-1, 1)$ to the curve with equation $y = 2x^3 - x^2 + 4$.

(Give your answer correct to $0 \cdot 1°$.)

Solution

Remember $m = \tan\theta$ from co-ordinate geometry.

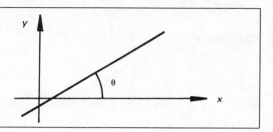

Here we need to find the value of the gradient of the tangent since

$m_{\text{tangent}} = \tan\theta$ where θ is the angle between the x-axis and tangent.

so $\theta = \tan^{-1}(m_{\text{tangent}})$.

Given $y = 2x^3 - x^2 + 4$

$$\Rightarrow \frac{dy}{dx} = 6x^2 - 2x$$

$$\therefore m_{\text{tangent}} = \frac{dy}{dx} \text{ at } x = -1$$
$$= 6(-1)^2 - 2(-1)$$
$$= 6 + 2$$
$$= 8$$
$$\therefore \tan\theta = 8$$
$$\theta = \tan^{-1} 8$$
$$= 82{\cdot}9°$$

4.1.4   INCREASING AND DECREASING FUNCTIONS

From section 4.1.3 you know that the derivative represents the gradient of the tangent to a curve.

If $f'(x)$ *or* $\frac{dy}{dx}$ is positive, i.e. > 0, the tangent is of the form / (i.e. a positive gradient) and so the function must be increasing

If $\begin{matrix} f'(x) > 0 \\ \frac{dy}{dx} > 0 \end{matrix} \Leftrightarrow$ function is increasing

If $f'(x)$ *or* $\dfrac{dy}{dx}$ is negative, i.e. < 0, the tangent is of the form $\diagdown$ (i.e. a negative gradient) and so the function must be decreasing

$$\text{If} \begin{array}{l} f'(x) < 0 \\ \dfrac{dy}{dx} < 0 \end{array} \Leftrightarrow \text{function is decreasing}$$

If a function is neither increasing or decreasing it is said to be stationary and $f'(x) = 0$ or $\dfrac{dy}{dx} = 0$

$$\text{If} \begin{array}{l} f'(x) = 0 \\ \dfrac{dy}{dx} < 0 \end{array} \Leftrightarrow \text{function is stationary}$$

Worked Example 4.8

For what values of x is the function $f(x) = x^3 - 12x + 2$ increasing?

Solution

$$f(x) = x^3 - 12x + 2 \Rightarrow f'(x) = 3x^2 - 12$$
$$= 3(x^2 - 4)$$
$$= 3(x + 2)(x - 2)$$

| $a^2 - b^2 = (a + b)(a - b)$ |
| Difference of two squares |

Function is increasing when $f'(x) > 0$.
So we require value(s) of x for which $3(x + 2)(x - 2) > 0$.

There are 2 methods of solving this, both of which are shown below.

Method I (most frequently used solution)

Table of Values

Step 1
Solve the equation $f'(x) = 0$
$3(x + 2)(x - 2) = 0$
$x + 2 = 0$ or $x - 2 = 0$
$x = -2$ or 2
$\therefore$ 'Critical values' are -2 and 2.

Step 2

Use a table of values (similar to that for curve sketching).

x	-2^-	-2	-2^+	2^-	2	2^+
$x + 2$	$-$	0	$+$	$+$	$*$	$+$
$x - 2$	$-$	$*$	$-$	$-$	0	$+$
$f'(x) = 3(x + 2)(x - 2)$	$+$	0	$-$	$-$	0	$+$

$\uparrow$ (under -2 column) $\qquad\qquad$ $\uparrow$ (under 2 column)

* This value does not matter

We require those values of x for which $f'(x) > 0$, i.e. the $+$ values from the last line of table.

Step 3

From the table deduce solution, i.e. $x < -2$ or $x > 2$.

Mathematically we write this as $\{x < -2 \text{ or } x > 2, x \in \mathbf{R}\}$

Method II

Algebraic Method

For a positive solution, i.e. $f'(x) > 0$ the 3 does not matter, we require

$\qquad$ $x + 2$ and $x - 2$ to be both positive **or**
$\qquad\qquad\qquad$ to be both negative.

$\qquad$ i.e. $3 \times (+) \times (+) = (+)$
$\qquad$ **or** $3 \times (-) \times (-) = (+)$

So $x + 2 > 0$ when $x - 2 > 0$
$\qquad$ $x > -2$ when $x > 2$
$\qquad$ i.e. $x > 2$

or $x + 2 < 0$ when $x - 2 < 0$
$\qquad$ $x < -2$ when $x < 2$
$\qquad$ i.e. $x < -2$

So $f(x)$ is increasing for $x < -2$ or $x > 2, x \in \mathbf{R}$

i.e. $\{x : x < -2 \text{ or } x > 2, x \in \mathbf{R}\}$

> Method I is less prone to error and easier to understand than Method II.

Worked Example 4.9

For what values of x is the function $g(x) = \frac{1}{3}x^3 - 3x$ decreasing?

> In this example and the next, only Method I will be used!

Solution

$$g(x) = \frac{1}{3}x^3 - 3x \Rightarrow g'(x) = x^2 - 3$$

Function is decreasing when $f'(x) < 0$.

Step 1

Solve the equation $g'(x) = 0$

$$x^2 - 3$$
$$= (x + \sqrt{3})(x - \sqrt{3})$$

$$x^2 - 3 = 0$$
$$x^2 = 3$$
$$x = \pm\sqrt{3}$$

> Leave as $\sqrt{3}$ and use this value in table unless otherwise stated.

Step 2

Table of values

x	$-\sqrt{3}^{\,-}$	$-\sqrt{3}$	$-\sqrt{3}^{\,+}$	$\sqrt{3}^{\,-}$	$\sqrt{3}$	$\sqrt{3}^{\,+}$
$x - \sqrt{3}$	$-$	$*$	$-$	$-$	0	$+$
$x + \sqrt{3}$	$-$	0	$+$	$+$	$*$	$+$
$g'(x) = x^2 - 3$	$+$	0	$-$	$-$	0	$+$
			$\uparrow$	$\uparrow$		

Step 3

Deduce solution from table.

$f(x)$ is increasing when $-\sqrt{3} < x < \sqrt{3}$

i.e. $\{x : -\sqrt{3} < x < \sqrt{3}, x \in \mathbf{R}\}$

Worked Example 4.10

For what values of u is the function $h(u) = \frac{2}{3}u^3 - \frac{3}{2}u^2 - 2u + 5$ increasing?

Solution

$$h(u) = \frac{2}{3}u^3 - \frac{3}{2}u^2 - 2u + 5$$

$$\Rightarrow h'(u) = 2u^2 - 3u - 2$$

$$= (2u + 1)(u - 2)$$

Function is increasing when $h'(u) > 0$.

Step 1

Solve $h'(u) = 0$

$(2u + 1)(u - 2) = 0$

$2u + 1 = 0$ or $u - 2 = 0$

$u = -\frac{1}{2}$ or 2

Step 2

Table of values.

u	$-\frac{1}{2}^-$	$-\frac{1}{2}$	$-\frac{1}{2}^+$	2^-	2	2^+
$2u + 1$	–	0	+	+	*	+
$u - 2$	–	*	–	–	0	+
$h'(u) = (2u + 1)(u - 2)$	+	0	–	–	0	+
	↑					↑

Step 3

Deduce solution from table.

$h(u)$ is increasing when $u < -\frac{1}{2}$ or $u > 2$

i.e. $\{u: u < -\frac{1}{2}$ or $u > 2, u \in \mathbf{R}\}$

4.1.5 CURVE SKETCHING

The derivative can also be used in the process of sketching the graph of a function. It helps to locate **stationary points** and to determine their nature.

Stationary points occur when $f'(x) = 0$

$$\frac{dy}{dx} = 0$$

There are three 'types' of stationary points.

(i)   Maximum turning point

(ii)   Minimum turning point

(iii)   Point of inflection   **or**

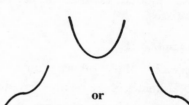

A table of values will determine the nature of each stationary point, i.e. what 'type' (i), (ii) or (iii) above each stationary point is.

Given the equation of any function, a sketch can be made by following the steps outlined below.

Step 1

Determine the point(s) where the curve cuts the x- and y-axes.

Remember curve cuts y-axis when $x = 0$, find $f(0)$.

curve cuts x-axis when $y = 0$, let $f(x) = 0$ or $y = 0$.

Step 2

Find any stationary point(s) and determine their nature.

Remember stationary points occur when $f'(x) = 0$ or $\frac{dy}{dx} = 0$.

Each solution identifies a stationary point whose nature can be determined by a table of values (as shown in the following examples).

Step 3

A very useful step!

Determine what happens to the function as x gets very large (i.e. $x \to \infty$) and as x gets very small (i.e. $x \to -\infty$).

This step will confirm that all stationary points have been found and that their natures are correct.

Step 4

The curve is now ready to be drawn.

If a **sketch** is required this can be done on blank paper and only the essential points found in Steps 1 and 2 need to be clearly shown.

If a **graph** is required this must be done on graph paper with appropriate scales for the axes.

Worked Example 4.11

Given the equation of the following curves find

  (i)   the co-ordinates of the points where the curve cuts the x- and y-axes;

 (ii)   the stationary points of the curve and determine their nature;

(iii)   sketch the curve.

(a) $f(x) = 5x^3(x-4)$ (b) $y = 2x^3 - 5x^2 - 4x + 3$

Solution

(a) (i) $f(x) = 5x^3(x-4)$

      Curve cuts x-axis when $f(x) = 0$

      $\therefore 5x^3(x-4) = 0$

      $x^3 = 0$ or $x - 4 = 0$

      $x = 0$ or 4

      $\therefore$ Curve cuts x-axis at $(0, 0)$ and $(4, 0)$.

      Curve cuts y-axis when $x = 0$, i.e. $f(0)$

      $\therefore f(0) = 5 . 0^3(0-4) = 0$

      $\therefore$ Curve cuts axes at $(0, 0)$ and $(4, 0)$.

(ii) | To find stationary point you have to find $f'(x)$ — need to expand $f(x)$ in order to calculate $f'(x)$.

$$f(x) = 5x^3(x-4)$$
$$= 5x^4 - 20x^3$$
$$\Rightarrow f'(x) = 20x^3 - 60x^2$$
$$= 20x^2(x-3)$$
$$\therefore 20x^2(x-3) = 0 \text{ at stationary points, i.e. } f'(x) = 0$$
$$\Rightarrow x^2 = 0 \text{ or } x - 3 = 0$$
$$\Rightarrow x = 0 \text{ or } 3$$

when $x = 0$, $y = f(0) = 0$ (from earlier investigations)

when $x = 3$, $y = f(3) = 5 \cdot 5^3(3-4) = -5 \times 27 = -135$

Stationary points occur at $(0, 0)$ and $(3, -135)$.

Nature

x	0^-	0	0^+	3^-	3	3^+	
x^2	+	0	+	+	*	+	* These values are
$x - 3$	–	*	–	–	0	+	unnecessary as
$f'(x) = 20x^2(x-3)$	–	0	–	–	0	+	$f'(x) = 0$ here.

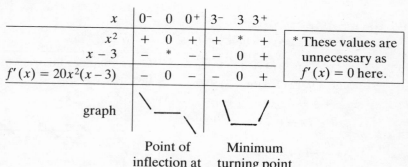

graph

Point of   Minimum
inflection at   turning point
(0, 0)   at $(3, -135)$

As $x \to \infty$, $y \to \infty$, $(\infty)^4 \to \infty$

(Graph slopes up as we go further along x-axis.)

As $x \to -\infty$, $y \to \infty$, $(-\infty)^4 \to \infty$

(Graph goes 'up' as we go further to the left along x-axis.)

| Dominant term in $f(x)$ is $5x^4$ — this will determine y as $x \to \infty$ and $x \to -\infty$

(iii) **Sketch**

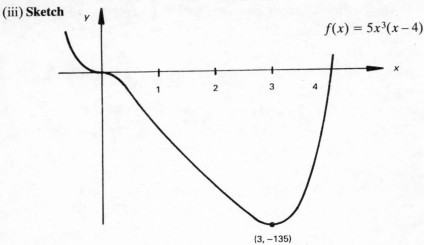

$$f(x) = 5x^3(x-4)$$

$(3, -135)$

(b) (i) $y = 2x^3 - 5x^2 - 4x + 3$

Curve cuts x-axis when $y = 0$

$2x^3 - 5x^2 - 4x + 3 = 0$

$\Rightarrow (x + 1)(2x - 1)(x - 3) = 0$

$\Rightarrow x + 1 = 0$ or $2x - 1 = 0$

or $x - 3 = 0$

$\Rightarrow x = -1$ or $\frac{1}{2}$ or 3

$\therefore$ Curve cuts x-axis at

$(-1, 0)$, $\left(\frac{1}{2}, 0\right)$ and $(3, 0)$

$\therefore$ Curve cuts y-axis when $x = 0$

$y = 2 \cdot 0^3 - 5 \cdot 0^2 - 4 \cdot 0 + 3$

$= 3$

$\therefore$ Curve cuts y-axis at $(0, 3)$

$\dfrac{dy}{dx} = 6x^2 - 10x - 4 = 2(3x^2 - 5x - 2)$

$= 2(3x + 1)(x - 2)$

Use remainder theorem to factorise cubic.

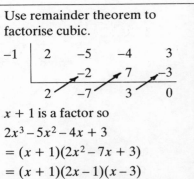

$x + 1$ is a factor so

$2x^3 - 5x^2 - 4x + 3$

$= (x + 1)(2x^2 - 7x + 3)$

$= (x + 1)(2x - 1)(x - 3)$

(ii) Since stationary points occur when $\frac{dy}{dx} = 0$

$2(3x + 1)(x - 2) = 0$ at stationary points

$\Rightarrow 3x + 1 = 0$ or $x - 2 = 0$

$\Rightarrow x = -\frac{1}{3}$ or 2

when $x = -\frac{1}{3}, y = 2\left(-\frac{1}{3}\right)^3 - 5\left(-\frac{1}{3}\right)^2 - 4\left(-\frac{1}{3}\right) + 3$

$\qquad = \frac{100}{27}$

when $x = 2, y = 2 \cdot 2^3 - 5 \cdot 2^2 - 4 \cdot 2 + 3$

$\qquad = -9$

$\therefore$ Stationary points occur at $\left(-\frac{1}{3}, \frac{100}{27}\right)$ and $(2, -9)$

Nature

x	$-\frac{1}{3}^-$	$-\frac{1}{3}$	$-\frac{1}{3}^+$	2^-	2	2^+
$3x + 1$	−	0	+	+	*	+
$x - 2$	−	*	−	−	0	+
$\frac{dy}{dy} = 2(3x + 1)(x - 2)$	+	0	−	−	0	+
graph	/	\		\	_	/

Maximum T.Pt at $\left(-\frac{1}{3}, \frac{100}{27}\right)$

Minimum T.Pt at $(2, -9)$

T.Pt $\equiv$ Turning point

As $x \to \infty, y \to \infty, (\infty)^3 \to \infty$

As $x \to -\infty, y \to -\infty \ (-\infty)^3 \to -\infty$

(These confirm what has been found previously.)

$2x^3$ is the dominant term in y and so will determine what happens to y as $x \to \infty$ and $x \to -\infty$

Remember

$(+ve)^3 = +ve$

$(-ve)^3 = -ve$

(iii) **Sketch**

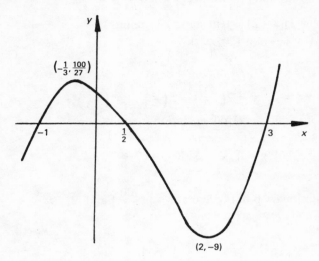

Worked Example 4.12

The diagram opposite shows part of the curve with equation $y = 9x + 3x^2 - x^3$

(a) Find the co-ordinates of the stationary points on the curve and determine their nature.

(b) If some line $y = k$ intersects the graph in 3 distinct points, state the range of values of k.

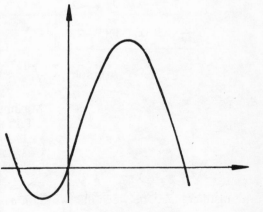

Solution

> We are not required to find the points where the graph cuts the x- or y-axes or to sketch the curve — need only do Step 2 of the curve sketching method.

164

(a) Given $y = 9x + 3x^2 - x^3$

$\Rightarrow \quad \dfrac{dy}{dx} = 9 + 6x - 3x^2$

$\qquad = 3(3 + 2x - x^2)$

$\qquad = 3(3 - x)(1 + x)$

Since stationary points occur when $\dfrac{dy}{dx} = 0$

then $\quad 3(3 - x)(1 + x) = 0$ at stationary points

$\qquad \Rightarrow 3 - x = 0$ or $1 + x = 0$

$\qquad \Rightarrow \quad x = 3$ or -1

When $x = 3 \quad y = 9 \cdot 3 + 3 \cdot 3^2 - 3^3 = 27$

When $x = -1 \quad y = 9(-1) + 3(-1)^2 - (-1)^3 = -5$

$\therefore$ Stationary points occur at $(3, 27)$ and $(-1, -5)$.

Nature

x	-1^-	-1	-1^+	3^-	3	3^+
$3 - x$	$+$	$*$	$+$	$+$	0	$-$
$1 + x$	$-$	0	$+$	$+$	$*$	$+$
$\dfrac{dy}{dx} = 3(3 - x)(1 + x)$	$-$	0	$+$	$+$	0	$-$
Graph	$\diagdown\_\diagup$			$\diagup\,\overline{}\,\diagdown$		
	Minimum T.Pt at $(-1, -5)$			Maximum T.Pt at $(3, 27)$		

(This is confirmed by the diagram at the start of the question.)

(b) $y = k$ is a horizontal line — it will only cut the graph in 3 different or distinct places between the two stationary points.

So $\quad -1 < k < 27$

> Note signs $<$ — do not use $\leqslant$ since line will only meet the graph in 2 distinct places for $k = -1$ and $k = 27$.

165

4.1.6 MAXIMA AND MINIMA

Differentiation, and in particular the method of finding the stationary points, can be used to determine when a **maximum** or **minimum** value occurs in order to obtain the 'best' solution to a problem.

The worked examples which follow show how this is done.

Worked Example 4.13

'The Smelly Place' Garden Centre has a model train which is used to show visitors around the many displays of flowers.

The cost per month, C pounds, of running the train is given by

$$C = 50 + 25V + \frac{400}{V}$$

Where V is the speed in miles per hour.

Calculate the speed which makes the cost per month a minimum and hence calculate this cost.

Solution

> Here we need to solve $\frac{dC}{dV} = 0$ for $V > 0$ and to find a minimum stationary point for one of the values — if there is more than one.

$$C = 50 + 25V + \frac{400}{V} = 50 + 25V + 400V^{-1}$$

$$\Rightarrow \frac{dC}{dV} = 25 - 400V^{-2} = 25 - \frac{400}{V^2}$$

At stationary points $\frac{dC}{dV} = 0$

$$\therefore 25 - \frac{400}{V^2} = 0$$

$$\Rightarrow \quad 25 = \frac{400}{V^2}$$

$$\Rightarrow \quad V^2 = \frac{400}{25} = 16$$

$$\Rightarrow \quad V = \sqrt{16} = 4$$

> Need only +ve $\sqrt{}$, −ve $\sqrt{}$ does not make sense.

Nature

V	4^-	4	4^+
$\dfrac{dC}{dV} = 25 - \dfrac{400}{V^2}$	$-$	0	$+$
graph	$\searrow$	$\_$	$\nearrow$

Minimum value occurs at $V = 4$

∴ Minimum speed is 4 miles per hour with a corresponding monthly cost of

$$50 + 25 \times 4 + \frac{400}{4} = 50 + 100 + 100$$

$$= £250$$

Worked Example 4.14

A channel for carrying cables is being dug out at the side of a road.

A flat section of plastic is bent into the shape of a gutter and placed into the channel to protect the cables.

If each piece of plastic measures 40 cm by 100 cm and folds occur x cm from each end.

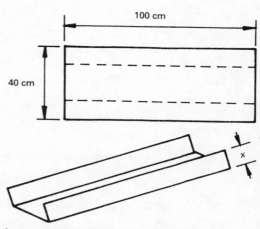

(a) Show that the volume $V(x)$ cm^3 of each piece of guttering is
$$V(x) = 200x(20 - x)$$

(b) Where should the fold be made to give the maximum volume and calculate this maximum volume.

Solution

(a) Volume = lbh

$$= 100(40 - 2x)x$$
$$= 100x(40 - 2x)$$
$$= 100x(2(20 - x))$$
$$= 200x(20 - x) \text{ cm}^3$$

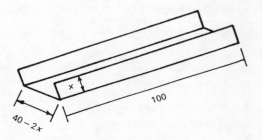

(b) When $\quad V(x) = 200x(20 - x)$

$$= 4000x - 200x^2$$

> Maximum volume occurs when $V'(x) = 0$

$$\Rightarrow V'(x) = 4000 - 400x$$
$$= 400(10 - x)$$

$V'(x) = 0$ when $400(10 - x) = 0$

$$10 - x = 0$$
$$x = 10$$

x	10^-	10	10^+
$V'(x)$	$+$	0	$-$
graph		$\diagup\diagdown$	

∴ Maximum volume occurs when $x = 10$.

∴ Folds should be made 10 cm from both ends.

Maximum volume $\quad V = (200 \cdot 10)(20 - 10)$

$$= 2000 \cdot 10$$
$$= 20\,000 \text{ cm}^3$$

4.1.7. TRIGONOMETRIC DIFFERENTIATION

The following rules can be added to those given in 4.1.2.

$$f(x) = \sin x \Rightarrow f'(x) = \cos x$$
$$f(x) = \sin ax \Rightarrow f'(x) = a \cos ax$$

This rule can be extended to

$$f(x) = \sin (ax + b) \Rightarrow f'(x) = a \cos (ax + b)$$

Worked Example 4.15

(a) $f(x) = \sin 3x \Rightarrow f'(x) = 3 \cos 3x$ | Here $a = 3$ |

(b) $f(x) = \sin \frac{x}{7} = \sin \frac{1}{7}x \Rightarrow f'(x) = \frac{1}{7} \cos \frac{1}{7}x$

$$= \frac{1}{7} \cos \frac{x}{7}$$

(c) $f(x) = 8 \sin x \Rightarrow f'(x) = 8 \cos x$

| Note here the constant is 'outside' $\sin x$ |

(d) $f(x) = -5 \sin 9x \Rightarrow f'(x) = -5 . 9 \cos 9x$

$$= -45 \cos 9x$$

(e) $f(\theta) = 4 \sin \frac{\theta}{8} = 4 \sin \frac{1}{8}\theta \Rightarrow f'(\theta) = 4 . \frac{1}{8} \cos \frac{1}{8}\theta$

$$= \frac{1}{2} \cos \frac{\theta}{8}$$

$$f(x) = \cos x \Rightarrow f'(x) = -\sin x \quad | \text{ Note '–' sign! } |$$
$$f(x) = \cos ax \Rightarrow f'(x) = -a \sin ax$$

As before, this rule can be extended to

$$f(x) = \cos (ax + b) \Rightarrow f'(x) = -a \sin (ax + b)$$

Worked Example 4.16

(a) $f(x) = \cos 11x \Rightarrow f'(x) = 11 \sin 11x$

(b) $f(x) = \cos \frac{x}{23} = \cos \frac{1}{23}x \Rightarrow f'(x) = \frac{1}{23} \sin \frac{x}{23}$

(c) $g(u) = 6 \cos 7u \Rightarrow g'(u) = 6 . (-7 \sin 7u)$
$$= -42 \sin 7u$$

(d) $p(t) = -5 \cos t \Rightarrow p'(t) = -5(-\sin t)$
$$= 5 \sin t$$

(e) $f(x) = -15 \cos \dfrac{x}{5} = -15 \cos \dfrac{1}{5}x$

$$\Rightarrow f'(x) = -15\left(-\dfrac{1}{5} \sin \dfrac{1}{5}x\right)$$

4.1.8 CHAIN RULE

To differentiate a function of a function, i.e. a composite function $f(g(x))$, the **chain rule** is the most appropriate and easiest way to do this.

In theory the chain rule is represented by

$$\frac{d}{dx}\big[f(g(x))\big] = f'(g(x)) \cdot g'(x)$$

or $\dfrac{dy}{dx} = \dfrac{dy}{du} \cdot \dfrac{du}{dx}$ where u is a function of x.

The rule in practice is shown below.

Worked Example 4.17

(a) $y = (x + 4)^2$

> With the chain rule there is no need to expand the bracket.

There are two 'techniques' commonly used — use the one which you find easier. (They are basically the same!)

Technique 1
$$y = (x + 4)^2$$

> Replace bracket by u

Let $u = x + 4 \Rightarrow \dfrac{du}{dx} = 1$

so $y = u^2 \Rightarrow \dfrac{dy}{du} = 2u$

$\therefore \dfrac{dy}{dx} = \dfrac{dy}{du} \cdot \dfrac{du}{dx}$

$$= 2u . 1 = 2u$$
$$= 2(x + 4)$$

Technique 2
$$y = (x + 4)^2$$

$$\Rightarrow \frac{dy}{dx} = 2(x + 4) \cdot \frac{d}{dx}(x + 4)$$

$$= 2(x + 4) . 1$$
$$= 2(x + 4)$$

> Here bracket is treated as single term. This derivative is multiplied by derivative of term(s) inside bracket.

In the following examples Technique 1 will be used.

(b) $\quad y = (x^2 + 4)^5$ | Let term(s) inside bracket be equal to u. |

Let $u = x^2 + 4 \Rightarrow \dfrac{du}{dx} = 2x$ | Differentiate u w.r.t. x |

so $\quad y = u^5 \Rightarrow \dfrac{dy}{du} = 5u^4$ | Differentiate y w.r.t. u |

$\therefore \dfrac{dy}{dx} = \dfrac{dy}{du} \cdot \dfrac{du}{dx}$

$\qquad = 5u^4 \cdot 2x$

$\qquad = 10xu^4 \qquad$ but $u = x^2 + 4$

$\qquad = 10x(x^2 + 4)^4$

(c) $\quad f(x) = (2x^3 - 5x + 7)^{7/2}$

so $\quad y = (2x^3 - 5x + 7)^{7/2}$

| Let $y \equiv f(x)$ |
| so $\dfrac{dy}{dx} = f'(x)$ |

Let $u = 2x^3 - 5x + 7 \Rightarrow \dfrac{du}{dx} = 6x^2 - 5$

so $\quad y = u^{7/2} \Rightarrow \dfrac{dy}{du} = \dfrac{7}{2}u^{5/2}$

$\therefore f'(x) = \dfrac{dy}{dx} = \dfrac{dy}{du} \cdot \dfrac{du}{dx}$

$\qquad\qquad = \dfrac{7}{2}u^{5/2} \cdot (6x^2 - 5) = \dfrac{7}{2}(6x^2 - 5)u^{5/2}$

$\qquad\qquad\qquad = \dfrac{7}{2}(6x^2 - 5)(2x^3 - 5x + 7)^{5/2}$

(d) $\quad f(x) = \cos^5 x.$ Let $y = f(x)$

$\qquad y = \cos^5 x = (\cos x)^5$

| Note that $\cos^5 x = (\cos x)^5$ |
| $\cos x$ inside bracket |

Let $u = \cos x \Rightarrow \dfrac{du}{dx} = -\sin x$

so $\quad y = u^5 \Rightarrow \dfrac{dy}{du} = 5u^4$

$\therefore f'(x) = \dfrac{dy}{dx} = \dfrac{dy}{du} \cdot \dfrac{du}{dx}$

$\qquad\qquad = 5u^4(-\sin x)$

$\qquad\qquad = -5 \sin x u^4$

$\qquad\qquad = -5 \sin x \cos^4 x$

| $u^4 = (\cos x)^4$ |
| $= \cos^4 x$ |

(e) $f(x) = 8 \sin^9 x \qquad y = f(x)$

        $= 8(\sin x)^9$

Let $u = \sin x \Rightarrow \dfrac{du}{dx} = \cos x$

so $\;\; y = 8u^9 \Rightarrow \dfrac{dy}{du} = 8 \cdot 9u^8 = 72u^8$

$\therefore f'(x) = \dfrac{dy}{dx} = \dfrac{dy}{du} \cdot \dfrac{du}{dx}$

        $= 72u^8 \cdot \cos x$

        $= 72u^8 \cdot \cos x \, u^8$ $\boxed{\begin{aligned} u^8 &= (\sin x)^8 \\ &= \sin^8 x \end{aligned}}$

        $= 72 \cos x \sin^8 x$

(f) By now you should realise Technique 2 is just a quick form of Technique 1.

    $f(x) = \cos^3 x - \sin^8 x$ $\boxed{\begin{aligned}&\text{Apply chain rule to both}\\ &\cos^3 x \text{ and } \sin^8 x \text{ in turn.}\end{aligned}}$

        $= (\cos x)^3 - (\sin x)^8$

$\Rightarrow f'(x) = 3(\cos x)^2 \cdot (-\sin x) - 8(\sin x)^7 \cdot \cos x$

        $= -3 \cos^2 x \sin x - 8 \sin^7 x \cos x$

        $= -\sin x \cos x (3 \cos x + 8 \sin^6 x)$

4.1.9   GRAPH OF THE DERIVATIVE

Do you remember the geometrical interpretation of the derivative? The gradient of the tangent to a curve.

We can use this fact to help draw the graph of $f'(x)$ given the graph of $f(x)$

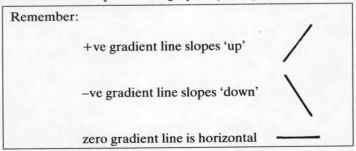

Remember:

    +ve gradient line slopes 'up'

    −ve gradient line slopes 'down'

    zero gradient line is horizontal

Worked Example 4.18

Given the graph of $f(x)$ below, draw the graph of $f'(x)$.

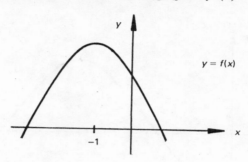

Solution

> The graph of $f'(x)$ will cut the x-axis at stationary points, since $f'(x) = 0$ at these points.

There is only **one** stationary point on the above curve $\Rightarrow$ graph will cut x-axis at **one point only**.

Stationary point occurs at $x = -1$ so graph of $f'(x)$ cuts x-axis at $x = -1$.

From $f(x)$

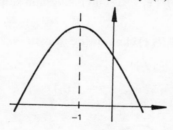

Left of $x = -1$
tangent slopes up
so $f'(x) > 0$.
(Graph of $f'(x)$ is
above x-axis.)

Right of $x = -1$
tangent slopes down
so $f'(x) < 0$.
(Graph of $f'(x)$ is
below x-axis.)

$\therefore$ Graph of $f'(x)$ is

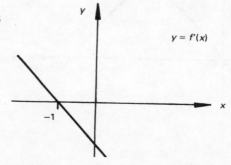

Worked Example 4.19

From the graph of $f(x)$ below draw the graph of $f'(x)$.

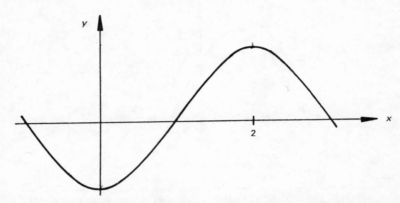

$f'(x) = 0$ at $x = 0$ and 2, i.e. stationary points, so graph of $f'(x)$ cuts x-axis at 0 and 2.

Graph is **above** x-axis when $f'(x) > 0$ (tangents/graph slopes up), i.e. for $0 < x < 2$.

Graph is **below** x-axis when $f'(x) < 0$ (tangents/graph slopes down), i.e. for $x < 0$ and $x > 2$.

The corresponding graph of $f'(x)$ can now be drawn.

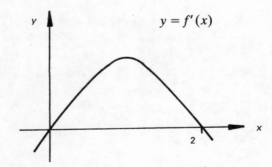

$y = f'(x)$

Worked Example 4.20

From the graph of $g(x)$ below, sketch the graph of $g'(x)$.

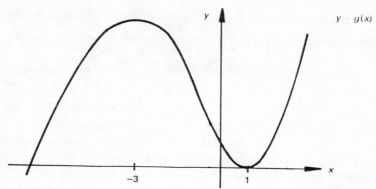

$g'(x) = 0$ at $x = -3$ and 1, i.e. stationary points, so graph of $g'(x)$ cuts x-axis at -3 and 1.

Graph is **above** x-axis when $g'(x) > 0$ (graph above slopes up),
i.e. for $x < -3$ and $x > 1$.

Graph is **below** x-axis when $g'(x) < 0$ (graph above slopes down),
i.e. for $-3 < x < 1$.

The corresponding graph of $g'(x)$ can now be drawn.

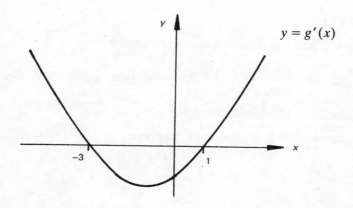

4.2 INTEGRAL CALCULUS

4.2.1 INTRODUCTION AND NOTATION

Integration can be thought of as the reverse process of differentiation.

The symbol for integration is $\int$ and there are two forms of the integral

Indefinite Integrals	Definite Integrals
$\int f(x)\,dx$	$\int_a^b f(x)\,dx$
No limits involved.	a and b are called limits.

Here the answer is almost always in the form of an algebraic expression and involves a **constant of integration**, C. (Some texts use k for the constant.)

Here the answer is always numeric and **does not** involve a constant of integration.

Some texts write

$$\int f(x)\,dx = F(x) + C \qquad \text{and} \qquad \int_a^b f(x)\,dx = F(b) - F(a)$$

to show these facts.

Note that for definite integrals.

If $a > b$ $\quad \int_a^b f(x)\,dx = -\int_b^a f(x)\,dx$

The lower limit is usually placed at bottom of $\int$ sign.

4.2.2 BASIC RULES

Like differentiation, there is a set of rules for integration.

I $\quad \int x^n\,dx = \dfrac{1}{n+1}x^{n+1} + C$, $n \neq -1$ and C is the constant of integration.

Worked Example 4.21 (Indefinite Integrals)

> These **must** include a constant of integration.

(a) $\int x^3\,dx = \dfrac{1}{3+1}x^{3+1} + C = \dfrac{1}{4}x^4 + C$

(b) $\displaystyle\int \frac{1}{x^2}\,dx = \int x^{-2}\,dx$ $\qquad$ $\boxed{\text{Note } \dfrac{1}{x^a} = x^{-a}}$

$\qquad = \dfrac{1}{-2+1}x^{-2+1} + C = -x^{-1} + C$

$\qquad\qquad\qquad = -\dfrac{1}{x} + C$

(c) $\displaystyle\int \sqrt{x}\,dx = \int x^{1/2}\,dx$ $\qquad$ $\boxed{\begin{array}{l} \sqrt[a]{x} = x^{1/a} \\ \sqrt{x} = x^{1/2} \end{array}}$

$\qquad = \dfrac{1}{\frac{1}{2}+1}x^{1/2+1} + C$

$\qquad = \dfrac{1}{\frac{3}{2}}x^{3/2} + C$ $\qquad$ $\boxed{\dfrac{1}{\frac{a}{b}} = \dfrac{b}{a}}$

$\qquad = \dfrac{2}{3}x^{3/2} + C$

(d) $\displaystyle\int x^{3/7}\,dx = \dfrac{1}{\frac{3}{7}+1}x^{3/7+1} + C$

$\qquad = \dfrac{1}{\frac{10}{7}}x^{10/7} + C$

$\qquad = \dfrac{7}{10}x^{10/7} + C$

(e) $\displaystyle\int \frac{dx}{\sqrt[5]{x}} = \int \frac{1}{\sqrt[5]{x}}\,dx = \int \frac{1}{x^{1/5}}\,dx = \int x^{-1/5}\,dx$

$\qquad = \dfrac{1}{-\frac{1}{5}+1}x^{-1/5+1} + C$

$\qquad = \dfrac{1}{\frac{4}{5}}x^{4/5} + C$

$\qquad = \dfrac{5}{4}x^{4/5} + C$

(f) $\int \dfrac{1}{x^{4/9}}\, dx = \int x^{-4/9}\, dx$

$$= \dfrac{1}{-\dfrac{4}{9} + 1} x^{-4/9\, +\, 1} + C$$

$$= \dfrac{1}{\dfrac{5}{9}} x^{5/9} + C$$

$$= \dfrac{9}{5} x^{5/9} + C$$

> Since integration is the reverse process of differentiation all of these can be checked by differentiating the answer.

II $\quad \int kx^n\, dx = k \int x^n\, dx = \dfrac{k}{n+1} x^{n+1} + C, n \neq -1$

k is a constant and C is the constant of integration.

Worked Example 4.22

(a) $\int 3x\, dx = 3 \int x\, dx$ $\qquad$ | Remember $x = x^1$ |

$$= \dfrac{3}{1+1} x^{1+1} + C$$

$$= \dfrac{3}{2} x^2 + C$$

(b) $\int 2\sqrt[3]{x}\, dx = 2 \int \sqrt[3]{x}\, dx$ $\qquad$ | $\sqrt[3]{x} = x^{1/3}$ |

$$= 2 \int x^{1/3}\, dx$$

$$= \dfrac{2}{\dfrac{1}{3} + 1} x^{1/3\, +\, 1} + C$$

$$= \dfrac{2}{\dfrac{4}{3}} x^{4/3} + C$$

$$= \dfrac{3}{2} x^{4/3} + C$$

$\dfrac{2}{\dfrac{4}{3}}$

$= 2 \div \dfrac{4}{3}$

$= {}^1\!\not2 \times \dfrac{3}{\not4_2}$

$= \dfrac{3}{2}$

(c) $\int \dfrac{dx}{3x^3} = \int \dfrac{1}{3x^3}\,dx = \int \dfrac{1}{3}\cdot\dfrac{1}{x^3}\,dx$ $\boxed{\text{Be careful with this type!}}$

$$= \frac{1}{3}\int \frac{1}{x^3}\,dx = \frac{1}{3}\int x^{-3}\,dx$$

$$= \frac{\frac{1}{3}}{-3+1}x^{-3+1} + C$$

$$= \frac{\frac{1}{3}}{-2}x^{-2} + C$$

$$= -\frac{1}{6}x^{-2} + C \left(= -\frac{1}{6x^2} + C\right)$$

$$\boxed{\begin{aligned}\frac{\frac{1}{3}}{-2} &= \frac{1}{3}\div\frac{-2}{1}\\ &= \frac{1}{3}\times\frac{1}{-2}\\ &= -\frac{1}{6}\end{aligned}}$$

(d) $\int -\dfrac{4}{3x^2}\,dx = -\dfrac{4}{3}\int \dfrac{1}{x^2}\,dx = -\dfrac{4}{3}\int x^{-2}\,dx$

$$= \frac{-\frac{4}{3}}{-2+1}x^{-2+1} + C$$

$$= \frac{-\frac{4}{3}}{-1}x^{-1} + C$$

$$= \frac{4}{3}x^{-1} + C \left(\frac{4}{3x} + C\right)$$

Note that

(i) $\int x\,dx = \dfrac{1}{2}x^2 + C$

(ii) $\int 1\,dx = \int dx = x + C$

(iii) $\int kx\,dx = k\int x\,dx = \dfrac{k}{2}x^2 + C$

(iv) $\int k\,dx = k\int dx = kx + C$

III $\int \big[f(x) + g(x) + h(x)\big]\,dx = \int f(x)\,dx + \int g(x)\,dx + \int h(x)\,dx$

Worked Example 4.23

(a) $\int (x^2 + 3x + 4)\,dx = \int x^2\,dx + \int 3x\,dx + \int 4\,dx$

$$= \frac{1}{3}x^3 + \frac{3}{2}x^2 + 4x + C$$

(b) $\displaystyle\int \frac{5x^3-7}{x^2}\,dx = \int \frac{5x^3}{x^2} - \frac{7}{x^2}\,dx$

$$= \int 5x\,dx - \int 7x^{-2}\,dx$$

$$= 5\int x\,dx - 7\int x^{-2}\,dx$$

$$= \frac{5}{2}x^2 + 7x^{-1} + C$$

$$= \frac{5}{2}x^2 + \frac{7}{x} + C$$

$$\boxed{\begin{array}{l} \dfrac{5x^3}{x^2} = 5x \\[2mm] \dfrac{7}{x^2} = 7x^{-2} \end{array}}$$

(c) $\displaystyle\int \frac{6x + 5x^{5/2}}{3\sqrt{x}}\,dx = \int \frac{6x}{3\sqrt{x}}\,dx + \int \frac{5x^{5/2}}{3\sqrt{x}}\,dx$

$$= 2\int x^{1/2}\,dx + \frac{5}{3}\int x^2\,dx$$

$$\boxed{\begin{array}{l} \dfrac{x}{\sqrt{x}} = \dfrac{x^1}{x^{1/2}} = x^{1-1/2} = x^{1/2} \\[2mm] \dfrac{x^{5/2}}{\sqrt{x}} = \dfrac{x^{5/2}}{x^{1/2}} = x^{5/2-1/2} \\[2mm] \hspace{2.2cm} = x^{4/2} = x^2 \end{array}}$$

$$= \frac{2}{\frac{1}{2}+1}x^{1/2+1} + \frac{\frac{5}{3}}{2+1}x^{2+1} + C$$

$$= \frac{2}{\frac{3}{2}}x^{3/2} + \frac{\frac{5}{3}}{3}x^3 + C$$

$$= \frac{4}{3}x^{3/2} + \frac{5}{9}x^3 + C$$

IV $\displaystyle\int (ax+b)^n\,dx = \frac{1}{a(n+1)}(ax+b)^{n+1} + C,\ n \neq -1$

C is constant of integration.

Worked Example 4.24

(a) $\displaystyle\int (3x+1)^2\,dx$ here $a = 3$ and $n = 2$

$$= \frac{1}{3(2+1)}(3x+1)^{2+1} + C$$

$$= \frac{1}{9}(3x+1)^3 + C$$

(b) $\displaystyle\int (2-7x)^3\,dx$ here $a = -7$ and $n = 3$

$$= \frac{1}{-7(3+1)}(2-7x)^{3+1} + C$$

$$= -\frac{1}{28}(2-7x)^4 + C$$

(c) $\int \dfrac{1}{\sqrt{x+5}}\, dx = \int \dfrac{1}{(x+5)^{1/2}}\, dx = \int (x+5)^{-1/2}\, dx$ here $a = 1, n = -\dfrac{1}{2}$

$\qquad = \dfrac{1}{1\left(-\dfrac{1}{2}+1\right)}(x+5)^{-1/2+1} + C$

$\qquad = \dfrac{1}{\dfrac{1}{2}}(x+5)^{1/2} + C$

$\qquad = 2(x+5)^{1/2} + C$

$\qquad = 2\sqrt{x+5} + C$

(d) $\int 6(5+3x)^{1/3}\, dx = 6\int (5+3x)^{1/3}\, dx$ here $a = 3, n = \dfrac{1}{3}$

$\qquad = \dfrac{\cancel{6}^2}{\cancel{3}\left(\dfrac{1}{3}+1\right)}(5+3x)^{1/3+1} + C$

$\qquad = \dfrac{2}{\dfrac{4}{3}}(5+3x)^{4/3} + C$

$\qquad = \dfrac{6}{4}(5+3x)^{4/3} + C = \dfrac{3}{2}(5+3x)^{4/3} + C$

(e) $\int \dfrac{2}{3(4-x)^2}\, dx = \dfrac{2}{3}\int \dfrac{1}{(4-x)^2}\, dx = \dfrac{2}{3}\int (4-x)^{-2}\, dx$ here $a = -1, n = -2$

$\qquad = \dfrac{\dfrac{2}{3}}{-1(-2+1)}(4-x)^{-2+1} + C$

$\qquad = \dfrac{2}{3}(4-x)^{-1} + C$

$\qquad = \dfrac{2}{3(4-x)} + C$

Worked Example 4.25 (Definite Integrals). **No constant of integration.**

(a) $\int_0^1 x \, dx = \left[\frac{1}{2}x^2\right]_0^1$

$\qquad\qquad = \frac{1}{2}\left[x^2\right]_0^1 = \frac{1}{2}(1^2 - 0^2)$

$\qquad\qquad\qquad = \frac{1}{2}(1 - 0) = \frac{1}{2}$

(b) $\int_{-1}^2 \frac{x^3 + 4}{x^2} \, dx = \int_{-1}^2 \left(\frac{x^3}{x^2} + \frac{4}{x^2}\right) dx$

$\qquad\qquad = \int_{-1}^2 x \, dx + \int_{-1}^2 4x^{-2} \, dx$

$\qquad\qquad = \frac{1}{2}\left[x^2\right]_{-1}^2 + 4\left[-x^{-1}\right]_{-1}^2$

$\qquad\qquad = \frac{1}{2}\left[x^2\right]_{-1}^2 - 4\left[\frac{1}{x}\right]_{-1}^2$

$\qquad\qquad = \frac{1}{2}\left(2^2 - (-1)^2\right) - 4\left(\frac{1}{2} - (-1)\right)$

$\qquad\qquad = \frac{1}{2}\left(4 - 1\right) - 4\left(\frac{1}{2} + 1\right)$

$\qquad\qquad = \frac{3}{2} - \frac{12}{2} = -\frac{9}{2}$

(c) Evaluate $\int_2^4 (2x^3 - 4) \, dx = \int_2^4 2x^3 \, dx - \int_2^4 4 \, dx$

$\qquad\qquad\qquad = 2\int_2^4 x^3 \, dx - 4\int_2^4 dx$

$\qquad\qquad\qquad = 2\left[\frac{1}{4}x^4\right]_2^4 - 4\left[x\right]_2^4$

$\qquad\qquad\qquad = \frac{1}{2}\left[x^4\right]_2^4 - 4\left[x\right]_2^4$

$\qquad\qquad\qquad = \frac{1}{2}(4^4 - 2^4) - 4(4 - 2)$

$\qquad\qquad\qquad = \frac{1}{2}(256 - 16) - (4 \times 2)$

$\qquad\qquad\qquad = \left(\frac{1}{2} \times 240\right) - (4 \times 2)$

$\qquad\qquad\qquad = 120 - 8$

$\qquad\qquad\qquad = 112$

Worked Example 4.26

The curve passing through (1, 4) has equation $y = f(x)$ and is such that $f'(x) = x(3x - 4)$.

Find the equation of the curve.

Solution

> Given $f'(x)$ we need to integrate to find $f(x)$, i.e.
> $$\int f'(x)\,dx = f(x) + C$$

Cannot integrate $x(3x - 4)$ as it is — need to expand brackets first.

$$\begin{aligned}
f(x) = \int x(3x - 4)\,dx &= \int (3x^2 - 4x)\,dx \\
&= 3\int x^2\,dx - 4\int x\,dx \\
&= 3\left[\tfrac{1}{3}x^3\right] - 4\left[\tfrac{1}{2}x^2\right] + C \\
&= x^3 - 2x^2 + C
\end{aligned}$$

From facts given curve passes through (1, 4) so

$$\begin{aligned}
f(1) &= 4 \\
\therefore f(1) &= 1^3 - 2 \cdot 1^2 + C \\
&= 1 - 2 + C \\
&= C - 1 \\
&= 4
\end{aligned}$$

so $C = 5$

and equation of curve is $y = x^3 - 2x^2 + 5$

4.2.3   TRIGONOMETRIC INTEGRALS

The following rules can be added to those given in section 4.2.2.

$$\int \sin x\,dx = -\cos x + C \qquad \text{Note } -\text{ve sign}$$

$$\int \sin ax\,dx = -\frac{1}{a}\cos ax + C$$

This rule can be extended to

$$\int \sin (ax + b)\,dx = -\frac{1}{a}\cos (ax + b) + C$$

Worked Example 4.27

(a) $\int \sin 5x \, dx = -\frac{1}{5} \cos 5x + C$

(b) $\int \sin \frac{x}{2} \, dx = \int \sin \frac{1}{2}x \, dx = -\frac{1}{\frac{1}{2}} \cos \frac{1}{2}x + C$

$$= -2 \cos \frac{x}{2} + C$$

(c) $\int 4 \sin 16x \, dx = 4 \int \sin 16x \, dx$

$$= -\frac{4}{16} \cos 16x + C$$

$$= -\frac{1}{4} \cos 16x + C$$

(d) $\int_0^\pi 3 \sin \frac{x}{3} \, dx = 3 \int_0^\pi \sin \frac{1}{3} x \, dx$ | Remember to use radians. |

$$= 3 \left[-\frac{1}{\frac{1}{3}} \cos \frac{x}{3} \right]_0^\pi \qquad \boxed{-\frac{1}{\frac{1}{3}} = -3}$$

$$= -9 \left[\cos \frac{x}{3} \right]_0^\pi$$

$$= -9 \left(\cos \frac{\pi}{3} - \cos 0 \right)$$

$$= -9 \left(\frac{1}{2} - 1 \right) = -9 \left(-\frac{1}{2} \right) = \frac{9}{2}$$

$$\int \cos x \, dx = \sin x + C$$

$$\int \cos ax \, dx = \frac{1}{a} \sin ax + C$$

As with the previous rules, this can be extended to

$$\int \cos (ax + b) \, dx = \frac{1}{a} \sin ax + C$$

Worked Example 4.28

(a) $\int \cos 8x \, dx = \frac{1}{8} \sin 8x + C$

(b) $\displaystyle \int \cos \frac{x}{10}\, dx = \int \cos \frac{1}{10} x\, dx$

$\displaystyle \qquad\qquad = \frac{1}{\frac{1}{10}} \sin \frac{1}{10} x + C$

$\displaystyle \qquad\qquad = 10 \cos \frac{x}{10} + C$

(c) $\displaystyle \int 3 \cos 9x\, dx = 3 \int \cos 9x\, dx$

$\displaystyle \qquad\qquad = 3 \left(\frac{1}{9} \sin 9x \right) + C$

$\displaystyle \qquad\qquad = \frac{1}{3} \sin 9x + C$

(d) $\displaystyle \int_{\pi/3}^{\pi/2} 2 \cos \frac{x}{2}\, dx = 2 \int_{\pi/3}^{\pi/2} \cos \frac{x}{2}\, dx$

$\displaystyle \qquad\qquad = \frac{2}{\frac{1}{2}} \left[\sin \frac{x}{2} \right]_{\pi/3}^{\pi/2}$

$\displaystyle \qquad\qquad = 4 \left[\sin \frac{x}{2} \right]_{\pi/3}^{\pi/2}$

$\displaystyle \qquad\qquad = 4 \left(\sin \frac{\pi}{4} - \sin \frac{\pi}{6} \right) \qquad \boxed{\sin \frac{\pi}{4} = \frac{1}{\sqrt{2}}}$

$\displaystyle \qquad\qquad = 4 \left(\frac{1}{\sqrt{2}} - \frac{1}{2} \right) \qquad \sin \frac{\pi}{6} = \frac{1}{2}$

$\displaystyle \qquad\qquad = \frac{4}{\sqrt{2}} - 2 \qquad\qquad \boxed{\frac{4}{\sqrt{2}} = \frac{4}{\sqrt{2}} \times \frac{\sqrt{2}}{\sqrt{2}}}$

$\displaystyle \qquad\qquad = 2\sqrt{2} - 2 \qquad\qquad\quad = \frac{4\sqrt{2}}{2}$

$\displaystyle \qquad\qquad = 2(\sqrt{2} - 1) \qquad\qquad\quad = 2\sqrt{2}$

4.2.4 GEOMETRICAL INTERPRETATION OF INTEGRATION

Geometrically, integration can be used to find

* the area under a line or curve
* the area between a curve and a line
* the area between two curves.

The following illustrate all of the possibilities that you will be likely to meet in the Revised Higher Mathematics examination.

Area under a line or curve

The shaded area can be calculated as

$$\int_a^b f(x)\, dx$$

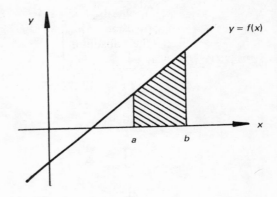

The shaded area can be calculated as

$$\int_a^b f(x)\, dx$$

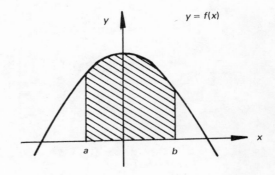

If the curve and area required is symmetrical about y-axis then:

$$\int_{-a}^a f(x)\, dx = 2\int_0^a f(x)\, dx$$

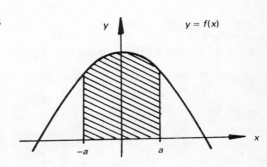

If the area being calculated lies wholly below the x-axis the final answer will be negative, e.g.

$$\int_a^b f(x)\, dx = -ve$$

> The area is found by taking the numerical value **without** the $-ve$ sign, i.e. the absolute value.

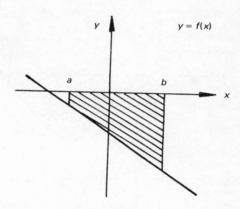

You must be careful with this type of integral as the following notes explain.

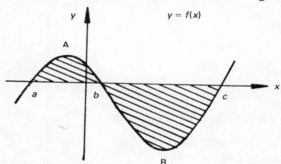

To calculate this shaded area **2 integrals** have to be evaluated

$A = \int_a^b f(x)\, dx$ **and**

$B = \int_b^c f(x)\, dx$

since $\int_a^c f(x)\, dx$ will give an incorrect value.

Why?

Area B would be negative and so $\int_a^c f(x)\, dx$ would give $A - B$ instead of $A + B$ required.

187

Similarly if the graph and area are symmetrical about the y-axis, two integrals are still needed, e.g.

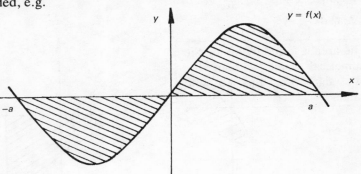

Shaded area $= -\int_{-a}^{0} f(x)\, dx + \int_{0}^{a} f(x)\, dx$

> This will be negative since area is below
> x-axis — hence – sign to make it +ve.

or by symmetry

shaded area $= 2 \int_{0}^{a} f(x)\, dx$.

Note that $\int_{-a}^{a} f(x)\, dx = 0$

since both areas are equal in size but opposite in sign.

Area between a curve and line

To calculate the shaded area in the
diagram opposite, find

$$\int_{a}^{b} f(x)\, dx$$

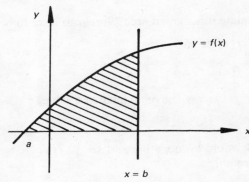

Similarly

To calculate this shaded area, evaluate

$$\int_a^b [f(x) - g(x)]\, dx$$

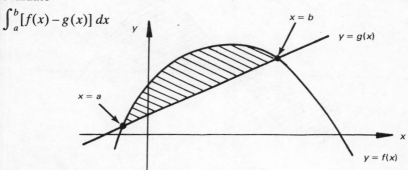

Here $f(x)$ is curve and $g(x)$ is line and since curve is 'above' line need to integrate $f(x) - g(x)$

Again, we know the points of intersection in this case, i.e. a and b. If the points of intersection are not known

$$f(x) = g(x)$$

must be solved before the **integral** can be calculated.

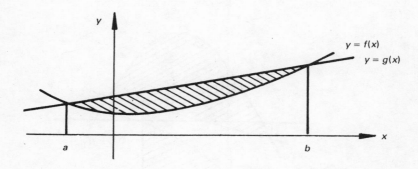

$f(x)$ is curve, $g(x)$ is line, line is 'above' curve.

$$\therefore \text{Area} = \int_a^b [g(x) - f(x)]\, dx$$

189

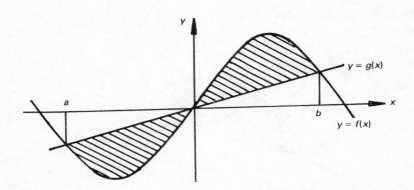

To calculate this area it is necessary to evaluate the integrals.

Area $= \int_{a}^{0} (f(x) - g(x))\, dx + \int_{0}^{b} (f(x) - g(x))\, dx$

If symmetrical about y-axis Area $= 2 \int_{0}^{a} (f(x) - g(x))\, dx$

There is no need to be concerned about the area here because part of the shaded area is below the x-axis.

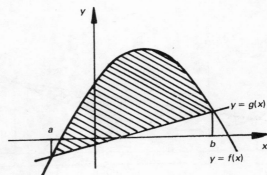

The area here is $\int_{a}^{b} (f(x) - g(x))\, dx.$

Area between two curves

The same rules as the previous section apply

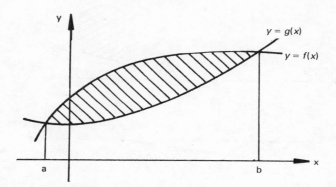

The graph of $f(x)$ is 'above' the graph of $g(x)$ so the shaded area is

$$\int_a^b (f(x) - g(x)) \, dx$$

Worked Example 4.29

Find the integral $\int_0^3 x^3 \, dx$ and make a sketch and shade the area represented by this integral.

Solution

$$\int_0^3 x^3 \, dx = \frac{1}{4} \left[x^4 \right]_0^3$$

$$= \frac{1}{4} (3^4 - 0^4)$$

$$= \frac{81}{4}$$

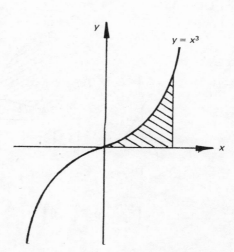

Worked Example 4.30

Calculate the shaded area shown in the diagram below.

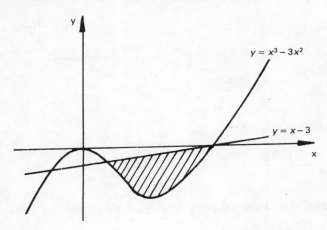

Solution

The points of intersection between curve and line must be found before the integral can be evaluated.

$$\therefore x^3 - 3x^2 = x - 3$$
$$\Rightarrow x^3 - 3x^2 - x + 3 = 0$$
$$\Rightarrow (x + 1)(x - 1)(x - 3) = 0$$
$$\Rightarrow x = -1 \text{ or } 1 \text{ or } 3$$

$$
\begin{array}{r|rrrr}
-1 & 1 & -3 & -1 & 3 \\
   &   & -1 & 4 & -3 \\
\hline
   & 1 & -4 & 3 & 0
\end{array}
$$

$$x^2 - 4x + 3 = (x - 3)(x - 1)$$

required integral

$$
\int_1^3 (x - 3 - (x^3 - 3x^2))\, dx = -\int_1^3 (x^3 - 3x^2 - x + 3)\, dx
$$

$$
= -\left[\int_1^3 x^3\, dx - 3\int_1^3 x^2\, dx - \int_1^3 x\, dx + 3\int_1^3 dx \right]
$$

$$
= -\left[\frac{1}{4}\left[x^4 \right]_1^3 - \left[x^3 \right]_1^3 - \frac{1}{2}\left[x^2 \right]_1^3 + 3\left[x \right]_1^3 \right]
$$

$$
= -\left[\frac{1}{4}(3^4 - 1^4) - (3^3 - 1^3) - \frac{1}{2}(3^2 - 1^2) + 3(3 - 1) \right]
$$

$$
= -\left[\frac{80}{4} - 26 - 4 + 6 \right]
$$

$$
= 4
$$

Printed and bound by Bell and Bain Ltd., Glasgow